DUKE·UNIVERSITY·PUBLICATIONS

Melville's Use of the Bible

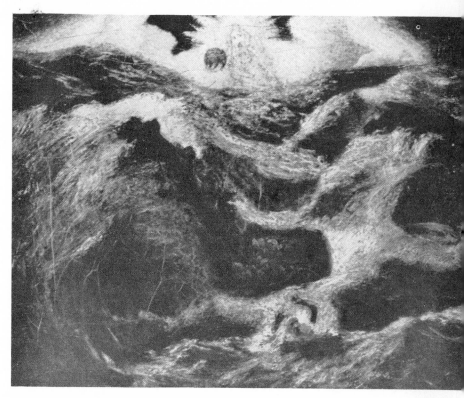

"Jonah" by Albert Pinkham Ryder

Melville's Use of the Bible

NATHALIA WRIGHT

WITH A NEW APPENDIX BY
THE AUTHOR

1969
OCTAGON BOOKS
New York

Reprinted 1969
by special arrangement with Duke University Press

OCTAGON BOOKS
A DIVISION OF FARRAR, STRAUS & GIROUX, INC.
19 Union Square West
New York, N. Y. 10003

To

STANLEY T. WILLIAMS

Contents

Melville's Use of the Bible

Introduction

THE LETTER which Melville wrote Evert Duyckinck comparing Shakespeare to Jesus and dating his discovery of the former in his twenty-ninth year is a remarkable picture in miniature of his literary character. Exclaiming over the large-print edition he had secured, he declared:

Dolt & ass that I am I have lived more than 29 years, & until a few days ago, never made close acquaintance with the divine William. Ah, he's full of sermons-on-the-mount, and gentle, aye, almost as Jesus. I take such men to be inspired. I fancy that this mount[?] Shakespeare in heaven ranks with Gabriel Raphael and Michael. And if another Messiah ever comes twill be in Shakespeare's person.[1]

His juxtaposition of the Bible and Shakespeare brings together the two major influences on his writing, and the common denominator he found between them illuminates his own pervasive moral purpose. Both were full of "sermons-on-the-mount." In both he read with sympathy the expression of a profound dualism, cleaving to the heart of creation yet thereby increasing its complexity and magnifying its wonder. The thought of both was couched in the early seventeenth-century idiom, the metaphysical strain of which is echoed in his most characteristic style.

[1] *Herman Melville: Representative Selections*, ed. Willard Thorp (New York, 1938), p. 370.

These influences, of course, were still germinating at the time Melville wrote Duyckinck in 1849, but their enormous effect upon him in maturity is presaged in his reference to his age. At twenty-nine he was reading Shakespeare for the first time. About the same date he became acquainted, through Duyckinck's library and his own European purchases, with Rabelais, Bayle, Marlowe, Jonson, Browne, Goethe, Carlyle, De Quincey, as well as with Emerson and Hawthorne, contemporaneous *voyageurs,* and the books ascribed to Solomon. His literary horizons suddenly widened in all directions, simultaneously with the burgeoning of his creative faculties.

To this lateness of date at which Melville began to read is due in part the complexity of relationships between his life, his reading, and his art. His introduction to literature, in unacademic sequence, followed rather than preceded his first brush with common life, which happened to be a rough and hazardous one. And partly because he brought to his reading nearly a decade of intense experience, he was able to make it come astonishingly alive and to assimilate it with unusual thoroughness. Between his physical and his mental activities there was never a gaping gulf.

Symbolic of this genuine coherence in Melville's literary character, and quite largely responsible for it, is the source which in his letter to Duyckinck sprang most readily to his command, constituting the touchstone of his judgment, furnishing the figure for his thought: the Bible. It was of all his sources, of course, the earliest and best known, the only one with which he was well acquainted before his late twenties, though through no determination of his own. But it was also one to which he deliberately turned and returned with the years. When a boy he heard its words as an inescapable part of his heritage; when a man he read it, as he read Shakespeare and Plato, for its message as well as its music. Its effect upon him was correspondingly deepened and prolonged, and throughout his mature repudiation of much of his environment it bound him fast to that environment, helping to save his thought from division.

The relationship between Melville's conservative background and the independent thought and mode of expression which he achieved for himself is, in fact, delicate. Though he rejected a good deal of the substance of that background, he retained many of its forms virtually intact. And though he was no more steeped in Scriptural tradition than many another of his generation, he drew upon it far more when he wrote than others of much greater orthodoxy.

The picture of his milieu is, indeed, an entirely familiar one. Both Gansevoort and Melville documents attest an inclination among his forebears to preaching and a general piousness in his immediate family.[2] Records of his own church affiliation are missing, but the circumstantial evidence of his novels is that he customarily attended worship on Sundays and that he listened to innumerable sermons. His brief schooling was in the "god-fearing" Albany Academy of Dr. Beck, where a course in *Historia Sacra* formed part of the regular classical schedule in the first year.[3] The city itself, a stronghold of piety and of Puritan economy, was his home from the time he was eleven until he was seventeen, a year before his first voyage. When he returned from the sea in 1844 he shortly married into a good Unitarian family, and throughout his adult years some of his closest friends were the Episcopal Duyckincks and their circle.

It was, to be discriminating, a background of middle-class morality rather than of religion, and to disengage the elements of the Biblical, the Calvinistic, and the socially conventional which composed it would hardly be possible.

[2] William Braswell, *Melville's Religious Thought* (Durham, N. C., 1943), pp. 4-8.
[3] Harold Larrabee, "Herman Melville's Early Years in Albany," *New York History*, XV (1934), 144-159.

Melville himself did not do so much. Indeed, perhaps the chief influence of his environment upon him was that it fostered, not his preoccupation with matters of morality and religion, but his inability to distinguish between the two.

Interested he was, not more from habit than from instinct, in the problems he heard discussed from his earliest childhood: the old, insoluble problems of what is good and evil, what is right and wrong. Though he could not accept certain of the solutions in vogue—such as the belief that virtue is rewarded by prosperity or that the civilization of Christian missionaries is an unqualified improvement upon a primitive Eden—he continued to argue the same questions, which vexed him, too, in the same terms, which he could not better. And all the while he perused an amazing variety of related literatures: the Bible; Biblical commentaries; the writings of major Christian dogmatists from Augustine to Calvin and of the more famous saints; Jewish history; Rabbinical and medieval religious lore; seventeenth-century sermons and metaphysical essays; the great Christian poets, Dante and Milton; comparative accounts of religions and mythologies; and, on the side of the opposition, the works of the stoics, the deists, and the skeptics.[4]

For all this interest in it, however, Melville's thought upon the subject of religion remained relatively immature. Though he speculated endlessly on the nature of God and on man's relationship to him, his implications were always ethical, his favorite presentation allegorical. A few members were for him the entire body. Of the church, of the great theological systems, of the teleological interpretation of history or of science, above all of the personal approach to the Deity—whom he often accused in the best Romantic

---

[4] Braswell discusses Melville's reading in or about many of these fields (*op. cit.,* pp. 12-16).

manner but never worshiped—he did not manifest a vestige of appreciation. The example of his contemporary Henry Adams, entering so completely into the complex religious consciousness of medieval man, affords a startling contrast.[5] Yet it may be this narrowness of Melville's religious concepts as much as his independence of dogma that determined his enormous debt to the greatest of religious books. Had he subscribed to an authoritative interpretation of Scripture he would scarcely have gone beyond perfunctory use of it. On the other hand, had any deep, personal religious experience been his, he should have been moved to language of greater immediacy, though of less association. In either case, he might have missed altogether what most authors do miss for one reason or another, though almost all have it opened to them: the Bible's unlimited artistic possibilities. As it was, Melville found this first of all his sources phenomenally the most wealthy, yielding history, literature, humor, speculation, spiritual exercises, a multiplicity of styles. And as he drew upon it, from the beginning to the end of his life, it became also the most influential of them all: the link between his inheritance and his achievement, between the abstruse philosophical problems he introduced in every book he wrote and the naturalistic scene and exciting plot which convoyed them.

No other contemporary of his so enriched his own pages. Beside him Emerson, with an actual ministerial career, and Hawthorne, preoccupied with the Puritan tradition, make slight and straightforward use of Scripture.[6] But Melville's mind seems to have been saturated with its stories, its ideas, its language. The allusions he made to it were not studied

[5] See Viola Chittenden White, "Symbolism in Herman Melville's Writings" (doctoral dissertation, University of North Carolina, 1934).

[6] See Harriet Rodgers Zink, *Emerson's Use of the Bible*, University of Nebraska Studies in Language, Literature and Criticism, Vol. XIV (1935); and John Cline, "Hawthorne and the Bible" (doctoral dissertation, Duke University, 1948).

but involuntary; they came from him spontaneously, as idioms in his vocabulary, as patterns of his thought. A man's private, even more than his public, writing may disclose such habits of reference, and so Melville's correspondence and his journal do. "Give ear then, oh ye of little faith," he exhorted Duyckinck apropos of the "resurection [*sic*] of Toby from the dead," and declared to him on the fourth day of a prolonged rain, "how much longer it is to last the ghost of the last man drowned by the Deluge only knows." To Hawthorne he wrote: "I feel that the Godhead is broken up like the bread at the Supper, and that we are the pieces." On his Mediterranean tour he observed, in a banal but favorite pun, that Constantine's soldiers were "sowed in corruption & raised in potatoes" and, more appropriately, that the descent into Avernus was "indication that he [man] sought darkness rather than light."[7]

With the same intimacy Melville echoed the Bible in novels, stories, and poems persistently from *Typee* in 1846 to *Billy Budd* in 1891—in every piece, in fact, of his collected work except five sketches and a few poems. Aside from the overtones of language and of thought inevitably accompanying such use of a source, there are upwards of fourteen hundred allusions to it alone, one, it may be estimated, on every seventh page of the prose and on every fourth page of the poems. For most of them are scattered through his pages. The story in which he may have intended concentrating the "Lore of the 'Bible,'" suggested by his night in Amsterdam "at the 'Old Bible,' upon which something good might be written in the ironical way,"[8] did not materialize.

There is, however, a notable fact about the distribution of these Biblical allusions. Their number mounted as Melville's career developed. By actual count they increase from

<hr>

[7] *Representative Selections*, pp. 368, 373, 395; *Journal up the Straits* (New York, 1935), pp. 27, 124.

[8] *Journal up the Straits*, pp. 39, 170.

a dozen in *Typee* to 100 in *Mardi* to 250 in *Moby-Dick* and then decrease, to rise again in *Clarel* to 600 and in *Billy Budd* to 100. A numerical estimate of them in proportion to the length of each volume is even more revealing, for thus arranged, his books stand in this order: *Clarel, Moby-Dick, Billy Budd and Other Prose Pieces, The Confidence-Man, Poems, Pierre, The Piazza Tales, Redburn, Israel Potter, White Jacket, Mardi, Typee, Omoo.* If *Clarel* is omitted, where the unusual number is due largely to the setting of the poem, there thus appears to be a correspondence between the most ambitious expressions of Melville's genius and his use of the Bible. The predominantly realistic tales are, significantly, toward the end of the list. It was in his most profound thought and his most distinguished style that he relied most heavily on Scripture.

But the picture is not yet complete. Dramatically corroborating the testimony of Biblical background in Melville's writing is the external evidence of the actual Bibles which he read. Two are preserved among the books he owned: the New Testament and Psalms presented to him in 1846 by his Aunt Jean Melville[9] and the family Bible inscribed "March 23ᵈ 1850 New York."[10] Both are plain issues, without notes or illustrations, unlike some of the embellished copies he delighted to describe; but like many of the items in his library they are largely interesting because of the marks of Melville's pencil which they contain. Most notable of all from a literary point of view, they are marks which accord in a remarkable way with the distribution of Biblical references throughout the books he wrote.

True, there are a few conspicuous discrepancies. Some of the passages to which he was most indebted bear no evidence of having been read in the Bibles he owned: the book of Jonah—except for a single verse, the story of Ahab

[9] In the Harvard College Library.
[10] In the New York Public Library.

in I Kings. At the same time, the apocryphal Wisdom of Solomon, which is not alluded to in all Melville wrote, is profusely marked and twice commented upon in the margin.

These exceptions aside, there is a general correspondence between the books of the Bible which Melville scored and commented upon and those which he quoted and alluded to. His markings, which occur in forty-four of the eighty books, are distributed rather evenly through the Old and New Testaments and the Apocrypha, though incidentally all but one of those in the New Testament were made in his separate volume of it. Within these three Scriptural divisions, however, certain books appear to have been distinctly his favorites. The one with the greatest number of verses marked, 77, is Psalms; next are Matthew with 52 and Isaiah with 51; then John, the Wisdom of Solomon, and Job, having 47, 46, and 45; afterward come Ecclesiastes, Genesis, I Kings, Jeremiah, Luke, I Corinthians, II Kings, and others having less than 10 verses marked. The list includes some of the books Melville cited most often when he wrote. For of the total number of his allusions two thirds are to the Old Testament, nearly a third to the New Testament, and about 15 to the Apocrypha. Of the 31 Biblical books unrepresented in his writing, 21 are not marked in his own copies. For the most part they are the minor prophecies, the most fabulous of the apocryphal writings, and the lesser epistles.

But there are far closer connections than these between the Bibles he read and the books Melville wrote. Some of his most often repeated allusions are to verses bearing the mark of his pencil: in Genesis the wars and destruction of the Cities of the Plain, the life and character of Jacob (in particular his dream at Luz); in Exodus the escape of the Israelites through the Red Sea into the wilderness; in the Books of Kings the fabulous wealth and wisdom of Solomon; wisdom sentiments in Job, Psalms, Proverbs, Ecclesiastes, II Esdras, Ecclesiasticus; the burning of Shadrach, Meshach, and Abednego in Daniel; Joel's valley of judgment; the Sermon on the Mount; John's vision of the Holy City.

Indeed, parts of *Moby-Dick, Pierre, The Confidence-Man,* and *Clarel* seem to have been written with one of these Bibles open beside the author. Jehovah's discourse to Job regarding the leviathan, which Ishmael quotes, is marked; so are other quotations which he makes from Proverbs, Isaiah, and Ecclesiastes; so also are the references to Ahaz's sundial and to the mulberries cast before Antiochus's elephants—verses of Scripture which provide two memorable figures of speech in the novel. In Luke, whose beatitude of woes seems to be the pattern for part of Father Mapple's sermon, one "woe" is noted. From Matthew both Pierre and White Jacket quote some of the very verses over which Melville paused, notably the admonition to turn the other cheek. *Pierre* also gives a prominent place to John's account of the woman taken in adultery; Melville had checked Jesus's reply to the scribes' accusation of her. *The Confidence-Man* opens with excerpts from the thirteenth chapter of I Corinthians and closes with the twelfth and thirteenth chapters of Ecclesiasticus. All three passages are penciled in Melville's Bible. As might be expected, however, it is *Clarel* which boasts the greatest number of Biblical allusions to marked verses, many of them containing uncommon details of scene and character: the slime pits of Siddim, the meeting of Abraham with King Melchizedek and his companions in the Valley of Shaveh, Abraham surveying the smoking Cities of the Plain, the "marching" Jehovah of Habakkuk, the theft of Achan, the sparrow alone on the housetop, the derision which Jeremiah sees heaped on Jerusalem when "All that pass by clap their hands."[11]

[11] Lam. 2:15. All quotations from the Bible, unless otherwise noted, are from the King James Version, which Melville used.

To watch Melville return thus to the language of orthodoxy to express what is often his most original thought is to pause and question his attitude to this source, so religious in content, appropriated to so literary an end. For if his use of it was not a perfunctory use, the reason was that his attitude was no perfunctory one. Whatever was the effect of his early indoctrination, by the time he wrote his major novels Scripture was " 'quite bereaved' " of any " 'Runic spell' "[12] for him.

So was it for many other contemporaries of Melville, though not for most of them. While the century on the whole upheld it to the end, here and there authority crumbled. Natural science, social science, a certain school of textual criticism itself assumed a generally secular view of Scripture, often in the process substituting new values for the rejected old ones. Of most of these rising influences Melville was well aware, and in this revaluation of the Bible he himself participated. Yet his attitude toward them was often curiously mixed.

The whole school of "Higher Criticism," for example, with its application of critical principles to Scripture, repelled when it might have attracted him. The German rationalism of its background and what he called the *"Coleridgean"* philosophy of being "free to inquire into Nature"[13] as well as into Scripture did stimulate his thought. But Strauss and Niebuhr thoroughly antagonized him. As might be expected, he was more disturbed by the effect of the new methodology on the New than on the Old Testament. His response to the whole school was, in fact, the fundamentalist one, though not for fundamentalist reasons.

---

[12] *Clarel*, II, 275. All references to Melville's works, unless otherwise noted, are to the Constable edition.

[13] Raymond Weaver, *Herman Melville, Mariner and Mystic* (New York, 1921), p. 285. In the MS of the journal the spelling is *"Colredegian."*

True, Melville's approach to the Bible was not uncritical, and in his reading of it he turned to various kinds of aids. But those he apparently relied on were of the conservative tradition. To elucidate "certain also of your own poets" in Acts 17:28 he added in the margin of his Testament "Aratus," and beside "a prophet of their own," Titus 1:12, he wrote "Epimenides." In the Twenty-ninth Psalm he identified Kadesh with Petra, and on the fifth verse he commented: "The storm begins in Lebanon & ends at Kadesh.—Stanley." The first two of these exegeses were to be found in the works of most eighteenth- and nineteenth-century Biblical commentators, such as Henry, Scott, Clarke, Jenks, Lange; and the last two come from Arthur Penrhyn Stanley's *Sinai and Palestine,* a copy of which he owned.

Similarly he attributed the Wisdom of Solomon to "some Alexandrian Jews" writing "a century before Christ," facts of composition agreed upon by such Scriptural dictionaries and encyclopedias as those of Kitto,[13a] William Smith, and McClintock. When he insisted, as he did in *Clarel,* on the allegorical nature of the Song of Solomon he was echoing the traditional interpretation of the book, much older in fact than Bernard of Clairvaux, to whom he ascribed it; among the higher critics it was being displaced by the Wetzstein-Budde theory that it is a collection of wedding songs. At the same time, however, Melville referred more than once to interpolations in this book, the controversial passages which are largely explained by the allegorical theory and which appear as extraneous chiefly in the light of Budde's research.

The truth is, of course, that Melville's use of Biblical aids, of whatever school, was neither sustained nor systematic. He did have an interest in texts and translations, evidenced both seriously and humorously in his books and his

---

[13a] For Melville's reliance on Kitto's *Cyclopaedia of Biblical Literature* in Chapter LXXXIII of *Moby-Dick,* see the edition of the novel with Introduction and Notes by Willard Thorp (New York, 1947), p. 342.

marginalia, but it was not altogether an intrinsic interest. He did not fill his pages with citations to chapters and verses, or rest on the authority of words. He even chose an early rather than a late reading if artistry dictated: the leviathan of Job he referred to constantly as a whale, despite its having been considered a crocodile for two hundred years. For simple dramatic value he preferred to call Moses the author of the Pentateuch, though since Spinoza the ascription had been questioned, and to date the creation 4004 B.C., contrary to the geological evidence he otherwise accepted.

For the Bible was literature to Melville as well as scripture; it was, in the somewhat trite words of the abbot in *Clarel,*

> "drama, precept fine,
> Verse and philosophy divine. . . ."[14]

And here he followed, more closely than he did in textual matters, in the general steps of contemporary students of the Bible, notably Lowth and Eichhorn, who were first to view Scripture as part of the body of Oriental literature. Among the marked passages in Melville's Bible are scores of the great Hebrew lyrics, which had, in fact, so roused Lowth's admiration: Deborah's song, David's dirge for Jonathan, Job's affirmation of faith, Isaiah's descriptions of Immanuel and of the suffering servant, Psalms 51, 121, 122, 137, Jesus's lament over Jerusalem. With full appreciation of the Bible's literary milieu, he spoke of " 'Orientalism's play' " in certain books, of " 'the Magi tincture . . . Derived from the Captivity,' "[15] and of the Egyptian influence on Moses.[16] Recognizing the inevitable problems of authorship in any age, he suggested that Solomon *"managed* the truth with a view to popular conservatism."[17]

---

[14] *Clarel,* II, 114.
[15] *Ibid.,* I, 295; II, 30.
[16] *Journal up the Straits,* p. 58.
[17] Letter to Hawthorne [June, 1851] (*Representative Selections,* p. 393).

Doubly interesting in this connection are his markings of Arnold's tribute to the literature of the Bible in his essay "On Translating Homer,"[18] for they throw light upon Melville's own stylistic debt to Scripture, a considerably greater one than Arnold's. He noted Arnold's words to the would-be translator: "He will find one English book and one only, where, as in the *Iliad* itself, perfect plainness of speech is allied with perfect nobleness; and that book is the Bible." Beside this dictum he drew triple lines and checks, and underscored the phrases here italicized:

The Bible, however, is undoubtedly the *grand mine of diction* for the translator of Homer; and, if he knows how to discriminate truly between what will suit him and what will not, the Bible may afford him also *invaluable lessons of style.*

The essayist's further advice to the translator to consult "the authority of the Bible" on questions of diction impressed him, and he both checked and underscored the confession: "My *Bibliolatry* is perhaps excessive."

All this is not to say, of course, that Melville altogether missed the religious significance of Judaism's and Christianity's Bible. Like most readers, he did search the Scripture for its metaphysical lessons. He pored over the writings of the prophets and the wisdom books, marked wherever they appeared verses treating of the accessibility of God, the nature of Jesus, damnation, immortality, predestination, and occasionally commented on them. In reply to Paul's exhortation, "Hast thou faith? have it to thyself before God," he noted, "The only kind of Faith—one's own."

Yet even here, at the very heart of Scripture, Melville continued to read with much the same kind of attention he gave all books. As he disentangled its truth from dogma he perceived it as akin to all other truth in the world. Hence

---

[18] Melville's copy of Arnold's *Essays* is in the Harvard College Library.

he was attracted by such comparisons as the one Friedrich von Schlegel made between the Bible and Indian philosophy, which he found mentioned in Robinson's *Diary*. He made similar comparisons for himself, noting that the ephod in Exodus was like the Catholic chasuble. And as he probed thus beneath its surface he arrived almost inevitably at what was for him the true religious significance of the Bible: its mythology, or its allegorical representation of metaphysical truth.

Here again Melville was in the stream, though probably without being aware of it, of notable nineteenth-century speculation. Anthropologists such as Frazer were furnishing the data with which magic and religion could be compared; the mission enterprise, at its peak, was discovering the characteristics of other beliefs; a growing conviction around the world that some unity underlay all cults was to culminate in the Parliament and Congresses of Religions at the Columbian Exposition in 1893. In Melville's case, however, it may well have been the theology in his background rather than his reading or his excursions among primitive peoples which started him on the way to recognizing in the Bible the great allegories of the Christian faith.

Still sensitive to that theology, Melville marked, toward the end of his life, the following sentences in his copy of Schopenhauer's *Studies in Pessimism:*[19]

Accordingly, the sole thing that reconciles me to the Old Testament is the story of the Fall. In my eyes, it is the only metaphysical truth in that book, even though it appears in the form of an allegory.

They are sentences which reassert in a remarkable way what Melville himself wrote in 1850 in his review of Hawthorne's *Mosses:*

[19] In the Harvard College Library.

Certain it is, however, that this great power of blackness in him derives its force from its appeals to that Calvinistic sense of Innate Depravity and Original Sin, from whose visitations, in some shape or other, no deeply thinking mind is always and wholly free. For, in certain moods, no man can weigh this world without throwing in something, somehow like Original Sin, to strike the uneven balance.[20]

The qualifying adjectives padding this opinion are calculated to save it from the appearance of doctrine. True, Melville gave no " 'Credence to Calvin' "[21] in any denominational sense, and in his copy of Emerson's *Essays*[22] he called the sage's thesis that all crime must issue in suffering "mere Theology—Calvinism?—The brook shows the stain of the banks it has passed thru." Yet the theological formula described phenomena which he perceived as elemental and inescapable. In turn, the Biblical passages from which such formulas were derived became for him mythology in the most profound sense.

It was on this point that Melville most thoroughly disagreed with the higher critics. In all his books the story of the Garden of Eden appears as the story of the essentially inward transition of the individual from innocence to experience. Its geography was without significance. Hence he objected to the efforts of scientists like Margoth to

"remand
Back from old theologic myth
To geologic hammers"

the land of Palestine, and to set such towns as Siddim " 'far From fable.' "[23] But his reason was the desire to preserve the deep wisdom embodied in the fable, rather than a fear for the Bible's external authority, and his bitterness lay in

[20] *Billy Budd and Other Prose Pieces*, p. 129.
[21] *Clarel*, II, 252.
[22] In the Harvard College Library.
[23] *Clarel*, I, 249.

his feeling that fact was being substituted for truth. The fate of Siddim and the Cities of the Plain was far more important than their site. Myth was superior to science, as the heart was to the head.

In much the same way he allegorized the New Testament. No strictly historical Jesus, as revealed by the Markan tradition, could be as moving as what the mind had made of him: a perfect nature, the idealism of whose ethic commanded adoration if not imitation. So he appears on all Melville's pages, a symbol of the state to which man aspires, as Adam is of the simplicity from which he rose. The historians as well as the geologists, complained Melville, "have robbed us of the bloom."[24]

How thoroughly literature and religion are mixed throughout this critique Melville himself knew, for his conceptions of both borrowed from each other. "It is with fiction," said he, "as with religion: it should present another world, and yet one to which we feel the tie."[25] The aesthetic, as enriching to the first category as it was impoverishing to the second, was not a new one. Emerson and Carlyle thought that the greatest literature is a kind of religion, and Herder's Spirit of Hebrew Poetry claimed for poet and prophet the same inspiration. Yet in a practice undiscovered by them, Melville employed the Bible symbolically and allegorically to effect a transition between the two realms and thus to capture the "ungraspable phantom of life."[26]

He was, in fact, anticipating a theory and practice shortly to follow him: the Freudian theory that the myth is the record of the racial unconscious and as such possesses spiritual value far superior to that of history. Its artistic value, in turn, can hardly be overestimated. For economy, for universality, for suspension of historical time, for depth and dignity of association the myth is not to be matched, as writers like Joyce and Mann have known. Indeed, Mann's great Joseph saga is an exploitation of one of the Old Testament themes best loved by Melville: the theme of exile and of its chastening power.

Thus deeply does the influence of the Bible on Melville go, beyond quotation and allusion, beyond allegory to true inspiration. For he did not depend for his effect upon the reader's awareness of his sources. Even in his earliest writing he turned their content into forms of his own and practiced for himself their formal principles. The effect on him of such books as Shakespeare and the Bible was remarkable for the reason that he not only echoed them verbally but re-created what he found there in terms of his own time and language, of his own vision. Their words sank to the deepest level of his consciousness, there to be constantly transforming and transformed by his thought and imagination.

CHAPTER II

Imagery

ALL MELVILLE'S WRITING from the realistic *Typee* onward is highly imagistic, and all his images have an interrelationship which constantly enhances their individual effect. His penchant for calling the names of remote lands and forgotten cities is scarcely separable from his fondness for the sea, nor his fondness for the sea from his sensibility to movement and to light and shadow. His preference for massive objects in nature is akin to his liking for kings and for gods. Akin to both is his use of hyperbole, and his exaggerations themselves lead eventually to his paradoxes.

Nor do Melville's Biblical images form a group distinct from all the rest. True, this is the aspect of his writing in which the influence of the Bible is most immediately apparent. But so largely a matter of general enrichment is it that there is hardly a topic, a sensibility, or a form manifest throughout his imagery which is not exemplified by Scriptural allusion. Even upon his titanic characters and his grand themes the effect is less extensive, though it may appear to be more significant. Yet as the imagery of any author reflects more clearly than the most direct exposition his principal interest, Melville's above all else reveals the extent and the depth of this influence upon him.

I

Considered as to content, his Biblical figures represent
a convergence of the two subjects most prominent in all
Melville's imagery: the antique and the marvelous. They
seem to have dominated his imagination, as light attracted
Bacon and as nature preoccupied Shakespeare. Probably
his interest in the former was fostered by the archeological
discoveries of the early nineteenth century, especially since
the most notable were in Egypt, Babylonia, and Assyria,
the ancient regions to which he most often alluded. The
names of Belzoni and Champollion occur in his figures of
speech, and Robinson's explorations in Palestine were
among those familiar to him.

At any rate, Melville handled these two subjects in his
imagery very much as a historian or an archeologist. That
is, he spoke not of the generally old or wonderful but of
actual men, countries, battles, books, and marvels of the
past. Among these proper names Scriptural ones are prominent, and in their selection may be seen the preferences,
unconfined to his Biblical material, which constitute the
individuality of Melville's images. Of Biblical places, he
preferred mountains and cities, especially ruined cities; of
persons, kings and spiritually gifted or supernatural beings;
of events, those of violence and those of vision or revelation.

Actually, except in *Clarel,* most of the place names on
Melville's pages have little geographical significance. The
words *Ararat, Tarsus, Bethlehem, Gaza, Gath, Uz, Sinai*
are as likely to call to mind a character as a place. And so
Melville meant them to do, when Redburn criticizes his
Liverpool guidebook for not pushing back to "the man of
Uz," and when Fayaway is said to prefer "the garb of
Eden."[1] With the names of still other places the association
is one of condition rather than topography. Tophet and
Gehenna mean hell; Cities of the Plain mean doomed so-

[1] *Redburn,* p. 190; *Typee,* p. 116.

cieties. "Let us freely enter this Golgotha,"[2] is White Jacket's way of introducing the subject of flogging through the fleet. Sacred and secular geography are allegorized together when Melville exclaims: "Out of some past Egypt, we have come to this new Canaan; and from this new Canaan, we press on to some Circassia."[3] Shinar, too, is emblematic, as the building of the bell tower is compared with the erection of the tower of Babel: "No wonder that, after so long and deep submersion, the jubilant expectation of the race should, as with Noah's sons, soar into Shinar aspiration."[4]

Generally more prominent in Melville's images than such places are persons, and most conspicuous of all are kings, whom he preferred above all men in or out of the Bible. In *Moby-Dick* alone the captain of the *Pequod* is compared to King Ahab and King Belshazzar; the harpooner Daggoo to King Ahasuerus, whom apparently Melville never identified with Xerxes; the fin-back whale, making a shadow on the water, to King Ahaz's sundial, for on "that Ahaz-dial the shadow often goes back."[5] The cone of another whale is likened to Queen Maachah's idol:

Such an idol as that found in the secret groves of Queen Maachah in Judea; and for worshipping which, King Asa, her son, did depose her, and destroyed the idol, and burnt it for an abomination at the brook Kedron [*sic*], as darkly set forth in the fifteenth chapter of the first book of Kings.[6]

Night cries heard by the *Pequod's* watch sound like the ghosts of King Herod's victims. Moby-Dick, maddened by the sight of the splintered boats, resembles King Antiochus's elephants when grapes and mulberries were cast before them. A passing whaler is named for King Jeroboam, and the masts of the *Pequod* itself stand up like "the spines

[2] *White Jacket*, p. 465.   [3] *Pierre*, p. 44.
[4] *The Piazza Tales*, p. 253.   [5] *Moby-Dick*, I, 171.
[6] *Ibid.*, II, 175.

of the three old kings of Cologne,"[7] as fable designates the magi.

Indeed, for all his democracy, Melville's world has an aristocratic cast. When invoking the spirit of equality his aim was not to degrade but to ennoble, to exalt the common multitudes, and to infuse the veins of all creatures with one royal blood. In so doing he more than once cited the Old Testament's genealogy of the race, as he did in Taji's exclamation:

King Noah, God bless him! fathered us all. Then hold up your heads, oh ye Helots, blood potential flows through your veins. All of us have monarchs and sages for kinsmen; nay, angels and archangels for cousins; since in antediluvian days, the sons of God did verily wed with our mothers, the irresistible daughters of Eve.[8]

So it is with Melville's supernatural world, which he peopled also with individuals of rank. Rolfe, observing Margoth gather geological specimens, declares that Milcom and Chemosh are scowling at him. As Clarel dreams of Ruth, who has shed a light in his room like that of the angel who released Peter from prison, he is as frightened as Eliphaz was at the spirit which passed before his face. The Arab troopers encountered by the pilgrims have the appearance at one time of the Witch of Endor, at another of the Carmel prophets. The palm tree is now addressed as a seraph, now as the Paraclete.

In addition to these Biblical types there were also a few individuals whom, judging by his repeated allusions to them, Melville preferred. They reappear in his pages in this order: Jesus, Jonah, Adam and Eve, Abraham, Solomon, Noah, Moses, Lazarus and Dives, Job, Samson, David and Goliath, Paul. Familiar as they are, they none the less exemplify his love of the erudite and the esoteric,

[7] *Ibid.*, I, 86.
[8] *Mardi*, I, 13-14.

since it is often one of the less familiar events of their lives
which is commemorated. Thus, Noah is repeatedly introduced imbibing wine (Judah is in " 'The true wine-zone of
Noah' "),[9] Paul buffeted by the wind Euroclydon, David
hiding in the Adullam cave (the sun is a hermit, "hutted in
an Adullum cave"[10]), Abraham entertaining angels. Jesus,
on the other hand, is most often pictured in some aspect of
his passion.

Of course, Melville was not always original, and on
occasion he treated individuals as the types which they
popularly represent: Anak and Og as giants, Cain and Abel
as participants in the first crime, the Hittites, Jebusites, and
Philistines as enemies. In Job, says Clarel, " 'Hamlets all
conglobe,' "[11] and to Nathan's ancestors the Indians were
Hittites. Jarl looks on Yillah as an Ammonite siren who
might lead Taji astray. A robin or a canary arriving among
the aquatic birds of Galápagos would be falling into the
hands of the Philistines. The Elizabethans are Anaks
among men. More than one South Sea island queen is
called a Jezebel.

Most of all, however, Melville's imagery was enriched
by the events of the Bible. Their tone varies considerably,
from God's walking in Eden in the evening to the confusion
of the Last Judgment. Yet, as Melville paused oftenest
before the grand aspects of nature and the most dramatic
moments of history, nearly all these events are of a spectacular nature. Many of them are miracles. Walking among
the cripples at the Liverpool dock, Redburn mused:

. . . I could not but offer up a prayer, that some angel might
descend, and turn the waters of the docks into an elixir, that
would heal all their woes, and make them, man and woman,
healthy and whole as their ancestors, Adam and Eve, in the
garden.[12]

[9] *Clarel*, II, 264.   [10] *The Piazza Tales*, p. 6.
[11] *Clarel*, II, 109.   [12] *Redburn*, p. 242.

In the course of compiling a list of the distinguished whale hunters of the past, Ishmael ingeniously proves first that the dragon which St. George vanquished was in all probability a sea and not a land creature, and finally that it was none other than leviathan himself:

In fact, placed before the strict and piercing truth, this whole story will fare like that fish, flesh, and fowl idol of the Philistines, Dagon by name; who being planted before the ark of Israel, his horse's head and both the palms of his hands fell off from him, and only the stump or fishy part of him remained.[13]

The Biblical incidents to which Melville repeatedly referred, however, fall into two groups: events of violence and destruction, and events of vision and revelation. Prominent among the retold stories of violence is the destruction of Sodom and Gomorrah, which he cited in describing such dissimilar objects and occurrences as the dismal Liverpool houses, those ships manned by what White Jacket considers evil crews, the sinking of the *Bon Homme Richard,* the ash box outside the Negro church in New Bedford, the sounds of the sharks tapping against the *Pequod,* and, in *The Confidence-Man,* all wicked thoughts. Other violent narratives recurring on his pages are those of Lot's wife, the Final Judgment, Jael's murder of Sisera, David's conquest of Goliath, Cain's murder of Abel, the drowning of the Egyptians in the Red Sea, Herod's slaughter of the innocents, the Crucifixion, the swallowing up of Korah by the earth. Avows Ishmael:

Preternatural terrors rested upon the Hebrews, when under the feet of Korah and his company the live ground opened and swallowed them up forever; yet not a modern sun ever sets, but in precisely the same manner the live sea swallows up ships and crews.[14]

[13] *Moby-Dick,* II, 103. See also *Poems,* pp. 62, 403, for other allusions to Dagon.
[14] *Moby-Dick,* I, 348.

The Biblical visions or revelations which Melville mentioned most often form almost as long a list as his favorite stories of violence. Among them are the dreams of Daniel and John, the Ascension, the Pentecost, the adoration of the seraphim, the appearances of angels and archangels. The waterspouts on the sea remind Taji of Jacob's ladder, descended and ascended by angels; and the deaf-mute in *The Confidence-Man*, because he is sleeping beneath the ladder leading to the next deck, suggests to his fellow-passengers that he is " 'Jacob dreaming at Luz.' "[15] In the poem "Art" Jacob's other angel visitant is introduced to propound an aesthetic theory in which hatred and love

> must mate
> And fuse with Jacob's mystic heart,
> To wrestle with the angel—Art.[16]

The sphere of the marvelous and the supernatural which Melville thus entered was not of course compassed by these Biblical events any more than his ancient world was peopled only by Hebrews. As his sacred verges on his secular history, so these stories blend with others as spectacular in his imagery: accounts of unusual natural phenomena, such as St. Elmo's fire and the phosphorescent ocean; excerpts from Greek, Egyptian, Norse, and Hindu mythology; excursions into the realm of memories, dreams, and the processes of thought. The series is infinite, its progression revealing each of his sources at more than one point.

II

More than content, however, composes the anatomy of imagery, and more than Melville's mental interests determined the individuality of his pictures of the sea, history, and the Bible. His sensibility also fashioned them. It was

[15] *The Confidence-Man*, p. 6.
[16] *Poems*, p. 270.

a sensibility first of all to movement, next to mass and line, finally to light.

Though all these qualities are of a visual nature, Melville's other senses were by no means undeveloped, as the abundant sensuousness of *Mardi* in particular testifies. He could smell the burning of Gomorrah and the pit; hear the trumpet in the Valley of Jehoshaphat, "the minstrels, who sang in the Milky Way"[17] at Jesus's birth, the "sounding brass" and "tinkling cymbal"; taste Belshazzar's feast; feel the heat of the fiery furnace. They are impressions whose quality is often extreme. His ear caught sounds audible only in the midst of a vast calm, as when he heard in *Billy Budd* the bony creak of the sea fowls' pinions. The scent of ambergris and the stench of the dead whale from which it comes afford a memorable contrast. Extremes of heat and cold, fire and ice, are his thermal stimuli. Hence part of the attraction which the story of Lazarus and Dives had for him was the contrast it represented between the coolness of Abraham's bosom and the infernal fires. The islands of Galápagos are personified:

Like split Syrian gourds left withering in the sun, they are cracked by an everlasting drought beneath a torrid sky. "Have mercy upon me," the wailing spirit of the Encantadas seems to cry, "and send Lazarus that he may dip the tip of his finger in water and cool my tongue, for I am tormented in this flame."[18]

But in general Melville's feeling for movement is keenest of all his sensibilities. The motion of waves, ships, clouds, fish, and aquatic birds often provided him with descriptive figures for entirely unaquatic scenes, while outside this sphere his figure of the loom captures the same restless spirit. The subject matter of a preponderance of the Biblical events he recalled involves violent movement: battles, burn-

[17] *Mardi*, I, 14.
[18] *The Piazza Tales*, p. 182.

ings, murders, flood, captivity, shipwreck, earthquake. White Jacket cites one such catastrophe as he complains of the tides, his figure, characteristically, appealing to opposite tactile senses at the same time:

During the pleasant night-watches, the promenading officers, mounted on their high-heeled boots, pass dry-shod, like the Israelites, over the decks; but by daybreak the roaring tide sets back, and the poor sailors are almost overwhelmed in it, like the Egyptians in the Red Sea.[19]

On a calm day, Ishmael observes, the sea "heaved with long, strong, lingering swells, as Samson's chest in his sleep."[20] So keenly did he perceive this movement of life that to Melville its absence signified spiritual death. It is the unceasing and inconclusive motion of the sea rather than the sea itself which constitutes his symbol for truth. So in *Mardi, Moby-Dick,* and *Clarel* the quiet water and the still air are oppressive, and the calm which pervades the scene is often a "dead calm." White Jacket distinguishes between the future and the past: "Those who are solely governed by the Past stand like Lot's wife, crystallised in the act of looking backward, and forever incapable of looking before."[21] Ahab, in the midst of a stillness which arouses melancholy speculations in him, cries: "'Would now St. Paul would come along that way, and to my breezelessness bring his breeze!'"[22]

Next to movement Melville was most sensitive to mass and to line. He spoke oftener of architecture and sculpture than of other art forms, of hills more than plains. *Pierre* is dedicated to Greylock Mountain, and *Israel Potter* to the Bunker Hill monument. Many of the Biblical places he named are themselves celebrated for some kind of form:

[19] *White Jacket,* p. 109.
[20] *Moby-Dick,* II, 326.
[21] *White Jacket,* p. 188.
[22] *Moby-Dick,* II, 38.

the Beautiful Gate, the gates of Gaza, the stones at Gilgal, the ladder at Luz, the Tower of Babel; neither Solomon's Temple nor the two-pillared temple of the Philistines was forgotten. The mountains of Scripture add their bulk to his pages: ". . . Romara flooded all Mardi, till scarce an Ararat was left. . . ."[23] His imagination saw giants even where there were none: the head of the slain whale is pictured hanging "to the *Pequod's* waist like the giant Holofernes's from the girdle of Judith."[24]

Often inseparable from this mass, in Melville's eyes, was line. All varieties of hieroglyphics, inscriptions, writing, tattooing, charts, labyrinths, and mazes interested him; among them were the twisted streets of Constantinople, the skeleton of the whale, the parts of the idol Dagon and the Beast of the Apocalypse, the handwriting on Belshazzar's wall, the mysterious lots called Urim and Thummim, the mark of Cain. The tattooing on the person of Lem Hardy combines sacred and profane lines: upon his chest was "a sort of Urim and Thummim engraven,"[25] and his forehead bore the figure of a blue shark, a mark which was

Far worse than Cain's—*his* was, perhaps, a wrinkle, or a freckle, which some of our modern cosmetics might have effaced; but the blue shark was a mark indelible, which all the waters of Abana and Pharpar, rivers of Damascus, could never wash out.[26]

A passage in *Mardi* characterizes Daniel not only as a prophet but a reader of inscriptions, as Taji and Jarl discover a barge of biscuit aboard the *Parki:*

Our castle the bread-barge was of the common sort; an oblong oaken box, much battered and bruised, and like the Elgin Marbles, all over inscriptions and carving:—foul anchors, skew-

[23] *Mardi*, II, 239.
[24] *Moby-Dick*, II, 37.   Nothing in the Bible indicates that Holofernes was a man of unusual size.
[25] *Omoo*, p. 38.
[26] *Ibid.*, pp. 32-33.

ered hearts, almanacs, burton-blocks, love verses, links of cable, kings of clubs; and divers mystic diagrams in chalk, drawn by old Finnish mariners, in casting horoscopes and prophecies. Your old tars are all Daniels.[27]

To light Melville seems to have been more sensitive than to color, and it is another testimony of his susceptibility to sensory extremes that he passed continually from brilliance into shadow and out again. Biblical Hebrew itself has few color words, and when he turned to the Bible for a description of this contrast he often found one ready made. The *Pequod* plunges, in the phrase of Jude, through "blackness of darkness" after Moby-Dick, who is as white as the robes worn by the twenty-four elders in Revelation. The volcanic mountain Narborough sends up smoke by day and flame by night, in imitation of the pillars of cloud and fire which led the Israelites through the wilderness. On the island of Juam the sun shines on one side of the mountain wall of the glen Willamilla, leaving the other side in darkness, while Taji fancies: "Thus cut in twain by masses of day and night, it seemed as if some Last Judgment had been enacted in the glen."[28]

Like the Hebrew poets, too, whose imagery of the sky he often marked in his Bible, Melville derived much of the light in his pages from allusions to the sun and the stars. In *Mardi,* where they lend support to Taji's fiction that he is a demigod from the sun, they are most noticeable, but other novels have their own astronomy. Exclaims White Jacket: "Quick! take the wings of the morning, or the sails of a ship, and fly to the uttermost parts of the earth."[29] The dawn in "Billy Budd" is compared to Elijah: "Like the prophet in the chariot disappearing in heaven and dropping his mantle to Elisha, the withdrawing night transferred its pale robe to the peeping day."[30]

[27] *Mardi,* I, 73.   [28] *Ibid.,* I, 253.
[29] *White Jacket,* p. 4.   [30] *Billy Budd and Other Prose Pieces,* p. 101.

As many of these figures suggest, the absence of light symbolized death to Melville, as did the absence of movement. This, too, is a conventional figure, which he sometimes gave doctrinal character by references to the "outer darkness," black Tophet, and the eternal night of the damned. " 'Blindness seems a consciousness of death,' "[31] observes Pani, the blind guide of Maramma, whose particular blindness recalls Jesus's epithet for the scribes and Pharisees: "Ye blind guides."

The absence of color, however, signified quite a different thing to Melville from the absence of light. If the meaning of the white objects he mentioned varies from book to book, and within a single book sometimes becomes too uncertain to have consistent symbolic value,[32] there is about them all a suggestion of the infinite. The blond Yillah is inscrutable; the white whale is uncapturable; the pockets, crevices, and voluminous folds of the white jacket are inexhaustible; the first, blond incarnation of the Confidence-Man—the deaf-mute—is uncommunicative; the fate of the fair, white-clad Billy Budd is inexplicable. Most of the Biblical white objects he cited actually touch the subject of immortality: Ezekiel's valley of dry bones (from which Benito Cereno's vessel seems launched), the leper Naaman, the apparel of the twenty-four elders, the fleece of the Lamb, the pale horse of Death.

That death itself was, in fact, less disturbing an idea to Melville than infinity is often suggested in his imagery. When, for example, the artist in the prose section of "Rip Van Winkle" encounters the lean moralist and his white horse he is reminded of the Evangelist's vision of Death on

[31] *Mardi*, II, 21.
[32] F. O. Matthiessen has pointed out how the symbolic values of black and white change, from the simplicity of *Typee*, *Mardi*, and *Redburn*, through the difficult imagery of *Moby-Dick* and *Pierre*, to the Agatha story, "Benito Cereno," and *Billy Budd* (*American Renaissance* [New York, 1941], pp. 502 ff.).

the pale horse. "A cadaver!" he exclaims, applying the epithet both to the horseman and to the near-by white church, and inevitably calling to mind the Scriptural phrase, "whited sepulchres." In contrast, however, he introduces an image not simply of life but of a distinctly human life, for he thinks of the temples of Greece, their marble mellowing with age and "taking on another and more genial tone endearing it to that polytheistic antiquity, the sense whereof is felt or latent in every one of us."[33] Far more awesome than the specter of death is the whole monotheistic tradition—unfixed by place, shadowed by a sense of imminent physical dissolution, looking to a disembodied life of the spirit.

Within the realm of life and humanity, however, certain colors do brighten Melville's pages, especially in *Mardi* and *The Confidence-Man*. Most of them are primary colors of brilliant hue, emanating, like his whiteness, from objects of symbolic value themselves. Brightest of all and most recurrent is red, especially the red of fire. "Fiery" is one of his commonest adjectives, and in *Moby-Dick* even a squall at sea is called a prairie fire. His allusions to the pit, the burning bush, the fiery furnace, the pentecostal tongues, the pillar of fire—all augment this effect. And all, because they represent excruciating trials of the spirit, have the peculiarity common among Melville's figurative fires: they burn without consuming. Ahab, whose fire worship has a Zoroastrian character, "looked like a man cut away from the stake, when the fire has overrunningly wasted all the limbs without consuming them. . . ."[34] The *Pequod* itself burns with corposants which do not destroy it, and which Ishmael compares to a Biblical scene in which fire actually has no part: ". . . seldom have I heard a common oath when God's burning finger has been laid on the ship;

[33] *Poems*, p. 328.
[34] *Moby-Dick*, I, 152.

when His 'Mene, Mene, Tekel Upharsin' has been woven into the shrouds and the cordage."[35] Even the whale must undergo an ordeal by fire; after being cut in pieces, he is at length "condemned to the pots, and, like Shadrach, Meshach, and Abednego, his spermaceti, oil, and bone pass unscathed through the fire. . . ."[36]

Most original of Melville's color schemes, however, is his use of green. Since the conventional "color" for innocence, white, represented to him something much more nearly ultimate, it rarely has this meaning in his pages. But in contrast there did exist in his imagination a connection between innocence or inexperience or primitive or domestic life and the color green. Truth is colorless, but the humanities are green.

The stages by which Melville arrived at this association are well marked. Green is "the peculiar signet of all-fertile Nature herself"[37] in contrast to the barren sea and the city, and therefore it is the emblem of the natural man in contrast to the restless inquirer after the universal secret. In moments when their thought wanders from the white whale, Ishmael speaks of the "grassy glades" and "ever vernal endless landscapes in the soul," and Ahab, swearing, " 'By the green land; by the bright hearthstone!' " avers his life to have been " 'the masoned, walled-town of a captain's exclusiveness, which admits but small entrance to any sympathy from the green country without. . . .' "[38] In Pierre's early ignorance of his father's character he maintains a white shrine for him in the "green bower" of his "fresh-foliaged heart," and when in subsequent disillusion he dreams of Enceladus he sees growing side by side beneath the Delectable Mountain the green, aromatic catnip and

[35] *Ibid.,* II, 279-280.
[36] *Ibid.,* II, 184.
[37] *Pierre,* p. 9.
[38] *Moby-Dick,* II, 264, 329, 328.

the colorless, inodorous amaranth—"man's earthly household peace, and the ever-encroaching appetite for God."[39]

The Biblical image which served Melville best in this connection was the image of Eden. He used it habitually to represent the life of innocence and felicity, and on occasion implied its color by calling the spot a greenwood, a glen, a garden, a neighborhood of "green Havilah."[40] How closely he associated it with domesticity, so important an aspect of the humanities to him, is evident from his coupling it with another favorite image: the hearth. Redburn confidently says of the new world: ". . . there is a future which shall see the estranged children of Adam restored as to the old hearthstone in Eden."[41]

Yet the earthly felicities which Melville often described in terms of greenness were to him less than the highest truth. Nostalgically dreaming of home, Ahab has a vision of the outworn scythe lying in the field—rusting " 'amid greenness.' "[42] For all his love of Saddle Meadows, Pierre's first mature experience compels him to depart; following him Lucy must see the vine, " 'the green heart-strings,' "[43] torn from her easel before it is transported with her. In the Biblical story the parallel continues: Adam, expelled from Eden, proceeds into the world with the knowledge of good and evil.

Since such symbolic values as these attach to so many of Melville's oft-repeated figures—ceaseless motion, ponderous bulk and intricate line, whiteness, fire, greenness—it is remarkable that his imagery has such strong sensuous properties as well. For the truth which he sought to represent was, he insisted, without body, color, odor, or sound; it could not be reached by the senses. Yet the movement,

[39] *Pierre*, pp. 93, 480. In Egypt Melville was struck with the same contrast: "Line of desert & verdure, plain as line between good & evil. An instant collision of alien elements. A long billow of desert forever hovers as in act of breaking, upon the verdure of Egypt. Grass near the pyramids, but will not touch them,—as if in fear or awe of them" (*Journal up the Straits*, p. 59).

[40] *Clarel*, I, 230.   [41] *Redburn*, p. 217.

[42] *Moby-Dick*, II, 330.   [43] *Pierre*, p. 443.

forms, and colors of his objects are among the richest and most memorable parts of his creation. In a characteristically Gothic method, he succeeded in defining reality by describing its masquerade.

III

Contrasted with Melville's fondness for experimentation elsewhere, the structure of his imagery is conventional. Metaphor, simile, and personification are his figures of speech, the catalogue and citation his other favorite devices. These forms are generally brief, loosely connected with the progress of the narrative, allusive rather than allegorical, pointing out a contrast at least as often as a comparison. Their simplicity insures their principal effect: the effect of the particular and the exalted rather than of the general and the common.

This desire to particularize, part of the Romanticism of his nature, accounts for the preponderance of proper names on Melville's pages, from scores of sources. The stomach of the whale does not resemble a cave, but the Kentucky Mammoth Cave; and whales swimming together in herds are like Hartz forest logs on the Rhine. Instead of referring to a gun, a grizzly bear, a miner, an elm, pebbles in the sun, a slave on an auction block, a king putting down a rebel, he speaks of a Colt revolver, a Missouri grizzly bear, a Cornwall miner, a Pittsfield elm, pebbles flashing in the Cuban sun, a slave up for auction in Charleston, King Richard overcoming Wat Tyler.

The same individualization is achieved by Biblical metaphor and metonomy. The conspicuously marked fin-back whale is the Cain of his race, and the albacore is the Nimrod of the seas. The continent of Africa in *Mardi* is represented by the island of Hamora. The sperm whale ordinarily produces but one of its kind at a time, but it has been known to give birth to an Esau and a Jacob. The priest

Aleema is described aboard his barge: "Meantime, old Aaron . . . sat, and eyed us."[44] Occasionally the allusion is suggested by the context, rising from it with appropriateness, even with inevitability. Redburn, describing the predicament of small craft at the mercy of larger fleets in the fog, personifies them with the remark: "Their sad fate is frequently the result of their own remissness in keeping a good look-out by day, and not having their lamps trimmed, like the wise virgins, by night."[45]

Most of Melville's allusions, however, are deliberately random. For he aimed thereby to suggest that, since almost any comparison would do, the original could be matched not once but hundreds of times. True, his catalogues, which bear out his intention, are often extremely monotonous on this very account, but at his best, by cutting all associations, he achieved a startling originality. The unusual and even the bizarre are no small parts of his imagistic effect. So, after witnessing Cuticle's amputation of the topman's leg, White Jacket declares that one day "life runs through us like a thousand Niles; but to-morrow we may collapse in death, and all our veins be dry as the brook Kedron [*sic*] in a drought."[46] The uncle in "The Happy Failure" thinks he spies a boy sitting like Zacchaeus in the tree across the stream—a story, incidentally, which Melville marked in his New Testament.

Of course, it must be remembered that such associations as these are not always as capricious as they seem, and that connections not visible on the page existed in Melville's mind. In a simile totally unprepared for, the sailors of the *Highlander*, deprived of their tobacco, are said to be as "inconsolable as the Babylonish captives."[47] But the inspiration for the figure may be contained in the second chapter thereafter, where Melville returned to the story of the captivity with more appositeness:

44 *Mardi*, I, 151.
46 *White Jacket*, p. 327.
45 *Redburn*, p. 124.
47 *Redburn*, pp. 353-354.

A sweet thing is a song; and though the Hebrew captives hung their harps on the willows, that they could not sing the melodies of Palestine before the haughty beards of the Babylonians; yet, to themselves, those melodies of other times and a distant land were sweet as the June dew on Hermon.

And poor Harry was as the Hebrews. He, too, had been carried away captive, though his chief captor and foe was himself; and he, too, many a night, was called upon to sing for those who through the day had insulted and derided him.[48]

Evidently the similarity which Melville saw between Harry and the Babylonian captives cast its shadow before, causing him to compare Harry's shipmates to the same group. The Psalm echoed in the longer passage is among those marked in his Bible.

Melville's chief fault in these brief figures was to be sometimes obscure, often grotesque. With characteristic fondness for the unusual he introduced unfamiliar verses without explanation and referred cryptically to familiar ones. Often the spirit of facetious journalism predominates. A captain, he suggested, interrogating a Portuguese as a prospective seaman, should inquire: "His knees, any Belshazzar symptoms there?"[49] One of the bachelors in the Temple desires a little more wine, just for his stomach's sake, like Timothy. Having to pay instead of being paid is an infliction of the two orchard thieves, and hell is an idea first born on an undigested apple dumpling. Pierre tells Lucy they will be married to the accompaniment of Job's trumpeters. Omoo enjoys his cube of salt beef and his hard biscuit after subsisting on the Nebuchadnezzar fare of the valley.

On the whole, Melville's more fully developed figures of speech, of whatever source, reflect greater discrimination on his part than the brief ones. They, too, particularize his material. But they also enlarge and elevate it by imparting

[48] *Redburn,* p. 358.
[49] *Billy Budd and Other Prose Pieces,* p. 272.

to essentially mundane persons and affairs significance far beyond that which they have in themselves. Thus, the common cock of Merrymusk, who was "more like the Emperor Charlemagne in his robes at Aix-la-Chapelle, than a cock" and whose evening crowing "went out of his mighty throat all over the land and inhabited it, like Xerxes from the East with his double-winged host," was also like "some overpowering angel in the Apocalypse. He seemed crowing over the fall of wicked Babylon, or crowing over the triumph of righteous Joshua in the vale of Askalon [*sic*]." He seemed to be saying, " 'Glory to God in the highest!' "[50] Vivenza, the land of promise, is likened to

St. John, feeding on locusts and wild honey, and with prophetic voice crying to the nations from the wilderness. Or, child-like, standing among the old robed kings and emperors of the Archipelago, Vivenza seemed a young Messiah, to whose discourse the bearded Rabbis bowed.[51]

The English sailor calls for a circle to be drawn about two quarreling sailors, but the Manxman, pointing to the horizon, exclaims: " 'Ready formed. There! the ringed horizon. In that ring Cain struck Abel. Sweet work, right work! No? Why then, God, mad'st thou the ring?' "[52] Melville watches from his piazza distant showers "which wrap old Greylock, like a Sinai, till one thinks swart Moses must be climbing among scathed hemlocks there. . . ."[53] The multitudes of sharks that swam round the sperm whale's body, as soon as his flesh was pierced, "rushed to the fresh blood that was spilled, thirstily drinking at every new gash, as the eager Israelites did at the new bursting fountains that poured from the smitten rock."[54] Viewing

[50] *Ibid.*, pp. 164, 153, 168-169. Melville must have meant Ajalon, to which he properly referred in *Clarel*, II, 247.

[51] *Mardi*, II, 175.

[52] *Moby-Dick*, I, 221.

[53] *The Piazza Tales*, p. 6.

[54] *Moby-Dick*, II, 54-55.

the unfortunate Bartleby's corpse, Melville quotes the words
of Job to a bystander:

> "Eh!—He's asleep, ain't he?"
> "With kings and counsellors," murmured I.[55]

In thus endowing his material with importance Melville
was not above purposeful exaggeration and even burlesque.
Addressing Duyckinck as "My Beloved," he implored him
to "come out from among the Hittites & Hodites."[56] White
Jacket's duff is as tough as the cock which crowed on the
morning Peter told a lie, and the whale smoke "smells
like the left wing of the day of judgment; it is an argument
for the pit."[57] Observing that the whale has no proper
face, Ishmael imagines his reply: "Thou shalt see my back
parts, my tail, he seems to say, but my face shall not be
seen."[58]

Nor did Melville forget the traditional method of giving
his words authority by the device of Scriptural citation.
Here again he sometimes parodied, but often he was in
earnest. White Jacket, discussing the order for all sailors
to cut their beards, refers to "the theocratical law laid down
in the nineteenth chapter and twenty-seventh verse of
Leviticus, where it is expressly ordained, *'Thou shalt not
mar the corners of thy beard.'*"[59] And in defense of the custom of dining at noon, he compiles a catalogue of Old
Testament characters:

Doubtless, Adam and Eve dined at twelve; and the Patriarch
Abraham in the midst of his cattle; and old Job with his noon
mowers and reapers, in that grand plantation of Uz; and old
Noah himself, in the Ark, must have gone to dinner at precisely *eight bells* (noon), with all his floating families and
farmyards.[60]

[55] *The Piazza Tales,* p. 64.
[56] Aug. 16, 1850 (*Representative Selections,* p. 380).
[57] *Moby-Dick,* II, 179.   [58] *Ibid.,* II, 123.
[59] *White Jacket,* p. 447.   [60] *Ibid.,* p. 35.

Of the Royal Mission Chapel of Papoar, which he calls "the chapel of the Polynesian Solomon," Omoo declares: "The materials thus prepared being afterward secured together by thongs, there was literally 'neither hammer, nor axe, nor any tool of iron heard in the house while it was building.' "[61]

This last comparison, as a matter of fact, did not originate with Melville, being contained in one of his chief sources for *Omoo*: William Ellis's *Polynesian Researches*. Here Ellis wrote:

It is probable, also, that, considering the Tahitians as a Christian people, he [the native king] had some desire to emulate the conduct of Solomon in building a temple, as well as surpassing in knowledge the kings and chieftains of the islands.[62]

The difference between this brief suggestion and Omoo's equally brief but bolder metaphor and citation is significant. Doubtless Melville found and duly appropriated a good deal of Biblical imagery in his secular reading, and it would be difficult indeed to say how many of his allusions were inspired by secondary sources. Certainly Stanley's *Sinai and Palestine* furnished some for *Clarel,* and the original Israel Potter document suggested the general Biblical parallel for that yarn. In such cases, however, Melville's method seems clear. It was to transform what he borrowed, extending and enlivening the original figure or substituting a more apt one.

To the Bible itself, in fact, Melville could be quite unfaithful, with the same simple artistic purpose. Sometimes it is his own connotation regarding a verse rather than the verse itself to which he alludes. A double image results: one perceives, in addition to the immediate object, not only a Biblical scene but one suggested by it which existed only

[61] *Omoo*, p. 199.
[62] London, 1833, II, 381. Quoted in Charles R. Anderson, *Melville in the South Seas* (New York, 1939), p. 223.

in the author's mind. So the old man whom the Confidence-Man meets at the end of his tale had "a countenance like that which imagination ascribes to good Simeon, when, having at last beheld the Master of Faith, he blessed him and departed in peace."[63] Though there is nothing in the Bible to describe Paul's voice, Redburn vows upon hearing the great bell-buoy in the Liverpool harbor: "I thought I had never heard so boding a sound; a sound that seemed to speak of judgment and the resurrection, like belfry-mouthed Paul of Tarsus."[64] When Thomas Fry boards the *Fidèle* he is "slanting his tall stature like a mainmast yielding to the gale, or Adam to the thunder."[65] The evening sun is likened to "the mild light from Abraham's tent"[66] and the fish following the *Chamois* are "tame and fearless . . . as the first fish that swam in Euphrates."[67]

The same kind of double image occurs when Melville referred to uncanonical variations on Biblical themes. He called by name the repentant thief—Dismas, and the three magi—Amerrian, Apelius, Damazon; and alluded to the Iron Crown of Lombardy, said to be made of a nail from the cross.[68] He cited the theory of the Rabbis that Jonah's whale was a female and that the devils as well as the sons of God intermarried with the daughters of men. In Ishmael's eyes the gentle rollings of the Pacific "seem to speak of some hidden soul beneath; like those fabled undulations of the Ephesian sod over the buried Evangelist St. John."[69]

IV

This predominantly artistic impulse behind all Melville's Biblical imagery is nowhere so clear as in *Clarel*, though in all his poetry that imagery is far less effective than

[63] *The Confidence-Man*, p. 321. [64] *Redburn*, p. 161.
[65] *The Confidence-Man*, p. 113. [66] *The Piazza Tales*, p. 139.
[67] *Mardi*, I, 172-173.
[68] *Clarel*, I, 324; II, 155; *Moby-Dick*, I, 209.
[69] *Moby-Dick*, II, 252.

in his prose. The shorter poems do not afford a very instructive comparison with the prose in this respect, since the imagery in both is introduced into generally similar contexts. But the content of *Clarel* is different. As the principal occurrence of the poem is a pilgrimage, undertaken by a man in the avowed hope of achieving a religious faith amid the scenes of that religion's birth, the imagery is largely predetermined. And since the poet's purpose is didactic, this imagery is never inappropriate or unelucidated, but it is often dull and obvious. There are fewer short, dramatic allusions to the Bible than there are in the prose, and more narratives are lengthily retold as the pilgrims come upon their original settings.

The fundamental contrast, in fact, which is necessary in all imagery is lacking in the use of Biblical allusion in *Clarel*. Underneath a superficial similarity there must be a permanent gulf, to be crossed by the imagination. In Melville's novels, tales, and shorter poems such a gulf exists between his secular or realistic material and the interspersed Biblical allusions, whereby an older, a weightier, and often a supernatural theme is suggested. In *Clarel* that contrast is not possible. Even if it be conceded that Melville's pessimism here is less religious than naturalistic, ethical, and political, and that it is the sins of all Western civilization which he has laid upon Christianity, the theme of the poem remains superficially religious, the setting deliberately Biblical. Images which in *Moby-Dick* or even in *Battle-Pieces* would be effective are obvious here. There is no element of surprise.

How fully Melville appreciated the value of contrast in imagery, however, is evident also in *Clarel*. Although the method he here pursued to achieve it differs from that employed elsewhere, it is an equally ingenious method, and had his purpose in writing been less argumentative it could have made the Biblical allusions in *Clarel* as effective as those in the main body of his work.

The contrasts achieved with Biblical imagery in *Clarel* are two. Biblical scenes are again compared with secular ones, but this time the immediate object is Biblical, the allusion secular. It is his earlier method reversed. Thus, Vine is pictured looking at

> the Crag of Agonies.
> Exceeding high (as Matthew saith)
> It shows from skirt of that wild path
> Bare as an iceberg seamed by rain
> Toppling awash in foggy main
> Off Labrador.[70]

The primitive hunter is called "Moccasined Nimrod, belted Boone."[71] Joshua battled his foes in a country which is like green Vermont. Tahiti is said to be the proper place for Jesus to have appeared in advent. The vision appearing to the shepherds at the time of his birth is compared with a phenomenon of nature:

> So (might one reverently dare
> Terrene with heavenly to compare),
> So, oft in mid-watch on that sea
> Where the ridged Andes of Peru
> Are far seen by the coasting crew—
> Waves, sails and sailors in accord
> Illumed are in a mystery,
> Wonder and glory of the Lord,
> Though manifest in aspect minor—
> Phosphoric ocean in shekinah.[72]

The other way in which Melville used Biblical imagery for contrast in *Clarel* was by juxtaposing it with pagan imagery, an economy in the pilgrims' lengthy discussions and a welcome dramatic relief. Especially Greek mythology is thus exploited. The flowers blossoming at the Sepulchre of Kings are

[70] *Clarel*, I, 229.   [71] *Ibid.*, II, 6.
[72] *Ibid.*, II, 190.

> Involved in dearth—to puzzle us—
> As 'twere thy line, Theocritus,
> Dark Joel's text of terror threading . . . .[73]

Celio, the crippled blond, has "Absalom's locks but Æsop's hump."[74] Ruth's is

> the grace
> Of Nature's dawn: an Eve-like face
> And Nereid eyes with virgin spell . . . .[75]

The Hellenistic Jews are characterized:

> "Recall those Hebrews, which of old
> Sharing some doubts we moderns rue,
> Would fain Eclectic comfort fold
> By grafting slips from Plato's palm
> On Moses' melancholy yew . . . ."[76]

Clarel's imagination is fired by the sight of the Syrian doves:

> It charmed away half Clarel's care,
> And charmed the picture that he saw,
> To think how like that turtle pair
> Which Mary, to fulfil the law,
> From Bethlehem to temple brought
> For offering; these Saba doves
> Seemed natives—not of Venus' court
> Voluptuous with wanton wreath—
> But colonnades where Enoch roves,
> Or walks with God, as Scripture saith.[77]

A striking use of metonomy and personification and one of the most dramatic of these comparisons occurs when Nehemiah envisages the Lamb of God:

[73] *Ibid.*, I, 111.   [74] *Ibid.*, I, 47.

[75] *Ibid.*, I, 67.

[76] *Ibid.*, I, 259. At the end of the Wisdom of Solomon in his Bible Melville wrote: "This admirable [?] book seems partly Mosaic & partly Platonic in its tone. Who wrote it I know not. Some one to whom both Plato & Moses stood for godfather."

[77] *Ibid.*, II, 143-144.

Last, dearer than ere Jason found,
A fleece—the Fleece upon a throne!
And a great voice he hears which saith,
Pain is no more, no more is death . . . .[78]

This interchange of symbols goes on also between Christianity and Egyptology, when Vine compares Jesus to Osiris; between Judaism and Zoroastrianism, when Cain and Abel are likened to Ormazd and Ahriman; between Judaism and paganism, when Clarel questions

Whether the lesson Joel taught
Confute what from the marble's caught
In sylvan sculpture . . . .[79]

The exception of such passages as these, with their philosophical content, makes all the more distinct the chief difference between Melville's sacred and his secular imagery: it is the infrequent use of Scripture in his strictly metaphysical figures, that is, in his embodiment of abstractions. For this purpose he employed general images such as the loom, the cave or mine or labyrinth, the isle, whereas he introduced most of his Biblical allusions in a context not of speculation but of the observation of specific physical phenomena.

Yet without exception they all serve his fundamental imagistic purpose, which was the expression of thought. It was, like that of the metaphysical school, not merely to ornament or to vindicate an idea but to give it form. If speculation about time or truth or security was best conveyed by naturalistic images, the appearance of the fleeting moment and of the changing scene was captured above all else by legend and by myth. In either case, to subtract Melville's image is largely to subtract his thought as well. The image is the essence of the thought—the allegory, the type, the emblem of its otherwise incommunicable nature.

---

[78] *Ibid.*, I, 325-326.   [79] *Ibid.*, II, 99.

CHAPTER III

Characters and Types

MELVILLE'S DRAMATIC SENSE, animating all his imagery, is not the sort, however, which creates objectivity in character. His people lead an interior existence. The details of their outward appearance are scanty, and the little inconsequential habits of action by which they might be made visible are missing. Types rather than individuals, they are "characters" in the seventeenth-century sense, embodying the most general states of mind: aspiration, utilitarianism, innocence. Simple rather than complex, they are variations of relatively few patterns. Compared with the infinite variety of Melville's images and of his style, the number of his character types and his themes is small indeed. Half a dozen at the most served him, as they served Hawthorne.

For about half these patterns the Bible provided prototypes: the type of Ishmael, of Ahab, and of Jesus. Because of the way Melville handled his originals, however, they account for some fifteen persons in his pages, and three ships. The relationships are simple. Redburn, White Jacket, Ishmael, Pierre, Israel Potter, Pitch, and Ungar are all Ishmaels. Ahab, Fedallah, Starbuck, Elijah, Gabriel, Macey, and the *Jeroboam* have counterparts in the story of Ahab in the first Book of Kings. Billy Budd and Pierre embody aspects of Jesus. Rounding out the cast, though loosely attached to it, are Bildad from Job, Nehemiah, the *Rachel* from Jeremiah, and the *Jungfrau* from the New Testament.

I

With the exception of three characters—Ahab, Benito Cereno, and Billy Budd—Melville's heroes are all essentially one person and have one prototype. He is Ishmael, the wanderer and outcast. The character of the wanderer is prefigured in the narrator of *Typee* and *Omoo,* the title of the latter signifying in Marquesan dialect a rover, or one moving from one island to another. Taji in *Mardi* is another rover, a symbol of the mind's pursuit of truth.

With Redburn the element of ostracism is added to the character. From their first meeting the callow Wellingborough is hated by his shipmate Jackson, a fact which sets so many of the crew against him that at last Redburn relates: ". . . I found myself a sort of Ishmael in the ship, without a single friend or companion; and I began to feel a hatred growing up in me against the whole crew. . . ."[1]

White Jacket, too, is subject to the taunts and jeers of his mates, principally on account of his conspicuous jacket. Regarding it as a symbol of misfortune, they lay the accidents of the voyage to its owner's account. True, he is not called an Ishmael, but it is perhaps not accidental that he acquires the name of another Biblical misanthrope when Priming cries: " 'Damn you, you Jonah! I don't see how you can sleep in your hammock, knowing as you do that by making an odd number in the mess you have been the death of one poor fellow, and ruined Baldy for life, and here's poor Shenly keeled up.' "[2]

Ishmael of the *Pequod* is the one character who bears the name of the common ancestor of them all. And with him the setting of the story assumes the prominence which it continued to have in Melville, at least as important as the

[1] *Redburn,* p. 79.　　　[2] *White Jacket,* pp. 418-419.

main character and often more so. The Biblical Ishmael is banished to "the wilderness of Beer-sheba" and grows up in the "wilderness of Paran," a phrase underscored in Melville's Bible. It is the solitary wastes of the sea, rather, in which the narrator of *Moby-Dick* wanders; or, in his own words, the "wilderness of waters." Periodically he flees the society of men, even though it offers him safety and joy. Like his shipmate Bulkington, he is impelled by some strange predestination to reject the lee shore for the "howling infinite,"[3] and thereby symbolically casts off all impediments in the pursuit of truth.

This brings Melville, in fact, to the very heart of the Ishmael story: the divine revelation to Hagar as she and her son languished in the desert. Before his birth Hagar was visited by an angel who instructed her to call the child *Yishma'el,* meaning "God shall hear." The name was a prophecy, fulfilled a few years later when, perishing of thirst in the desert, he was saved by the miraculous appearance of a well of water. On this occasion an angel spoke again to Hagar.

Except for the element of deliverance, which he associated with illusion rather than reality, this is Melville's allegory. Truth is to be sought in the solitary wilderness. In his imagination the waste place and the green landscape are symbols—in *Mardi, Moby-Dick, Pierre, Clarel.* The illusory haunt of truth, or superficial truth, is the oasis, the verdant isle, the secure land, the fertile field, the sweetness of society and domesticity. These are safe and felicitous; these are attainable. But reality itself, the abstract and the ultimate, resides in the wilderness, whether of land or of sea;[4] in the unhuman, indefinite, perilous waste.

[3] *Moby-Dick,* I, 133.
[4] In his copy of the New Testament Melville wrote beside Matt. 13:2 the words "The Sea." The verse describes Jesus teaching from a boat on the lake of Galilee, an association of the truth with a body of water which Melville himself was so fond of making.

That is, it is to be found here if it is to be found any-
where. The going is lonely and rough, but, harshest fact of
all, the end may never be reached. For Melville's heroes,
like the knights of medieval romance, are engaged in a
quest rather than an achievement. In the wilderness through
which they pass no divine voice speaks, as it spoke to Hagar.
But here the unanswerable question is asked. It is a place
of revelation. And if nothing more is revealed than that
the nature of reality is like the nature of the desert—vast,
voiceless, and fearful—that is itself a mature, a profound,
and a positive discovery.

Now, whatever its source, Melville's is not the conventional meaning attached to the symbol of the sterile wasteland. True, the impersonality of truth was being pressed
upon his generation by such biologists and geologists as
Darwin and Lyell, whom he read. He even found the
image of the desert in a book or two in his library, where
he penciled the passages. Disraeli in *The Literary Character of Men of Genius* had written: "This desert of solitude,
so vast and so dreary to the man of the world, to the man
of genius is the magical garden of Armida, whose enchantments arose amidst solitude, while solitude was everywhere
among those enchantments." With a touch of religious
fervor Balzac had imagined Brother Albert writing to the
Abbé de Grancey: " 'Misfortune creates in some souls a
vast desert in which the Divine Voice resounds.' " The
quotation Melville found in Walker's *Comédie Humaine
and Its Author.*[5]

But in the Bible the desert or wilderness is a common
setting for a vision of one kind or another. The Exodus
itself in the history of the Hebrews represents the closest
communion they ever had with Jehovah. Surely mindful
of that fact, Melville marked in his Bible several verses
referring to the wilderness in which they sojourned,[6] and

[5] Melville's copies of both books are in the New York Public Library.
[6] Exod. 3:1; 13:18, 20; Jer. 2:2, 6.

also marked similar descriptive passages in Stanley's *Sinai and Palestine*. He knew, too, of the connection established by both Testaments between a life in the wilderness and the ability to prophesy: John the Baptist emerged from the desert to preach, and Jesus retired into it for spiritual enlightenment. It was a phenomenon to which he referred more than once: in *Clarel,* in *Billy Budd*. He underscored in Matthew 3:3 the words: "The voice of one crying in the wilderness," and concluded in his speculations "Of Deserts":

> But to pure hearts it yields no fear;
> And John, he found wild honey here.[7]

In his Journal he shuddered at the Judean landscape which, he thought, "must have suggested to the Jewish prophets, their ghastly theology," but he added: "Is the desolation of the land the result of the fatal embrace of the Deity? Hapless are the favorites of Heaven."[8]

In the Old Testament, moreover, the idea of revelation is sometimes associated with particular places, and repeatedly with the vicinity of Beer-sheba, whither Hagar and Ishmael were banished. It was an important holy place in Hebrew history, where theophanies were frequently vouchsafed. Here Jehovah spoke to Hagar, Isaac, Jacob, and Elijah. In the stories of Hagar and of Elijah, favorites of Melville's, the scene is specifically "the wilderness" outside the town.

This episode of Ishmael's deliverance at Beer-sheba is the basis for one more analogy between his story and that of *Moby-Dick's* narrator. Both seem to lead charmed lives, though among Melville's heroes Ishmael is unusual in this respect. As Hagar's son was saved by a miracle from a death in the desert, so with the wreck of the *Pequod* only the sailor Ishmael escapes, and that by a margin so narrow

[7] *Clarel*, I, 217.
[8] *Journal up the Straits*, pp. 88, 92.

as to seem miraculous. This is a parallel unacknowledged by Melville's actual text. But the survival of Ishmael the sailor is linked with that of another Biblical character, Job's servant, whose words are affixed to the Epilogue: "And I only am escaped to tell thee." Again two Biblical types seem to have been interchangeable in Melville's mind, as Jonah and Ishmael were in *White Jacket*.

Pierre is still another Ishmael, driven like the *Pequod's* Ishmael by desperate necessity to spurn his old human associations and to proceed alone in his quest for truth. In acknowledging his new-found sister he must abandon his mother and his fiancée; he, too, must "embrace the boundless and the unbodied air."[9] So he leaves the green country of Saddle Meadows for the colorless and unhuman city, which significantly is a seaport.

The relationship, in fact, between Melville's country and city resembles that between his water and land, and the same figure is used to describe both city and sea: Pierre flees to one of the modern Babylonian "wildernesses of tiles, slate, shingles, and tin."[10] Earlier his exile is described in terms of Ishmael's wilderness, when, contemplating his plan to feign marriage with Isabel, he temporarily recoils from it: "Fain, then, for one moment, would he have recalled the thousand sweet illusions of Life; though purchased at the price of Life's Truth; so that once more he might not feel himself driven out an infant Ishmael into the desert, with no maternal Hagar to accompany and comfort him."[11] For in his story Mrs. Glendinning corresponds not to Hagar but to Sarah, who is the cause of the illegitimate child's being dismissed from the Abrahamic household.

[9] *Pierre*, p. 252.
[10] *Ibid.*, p. 377. In his copy of Alger's *Solitudes of Nature and of Man* Melville checked these lines of Maurice de Guérin: "Which is the true God? The God of cities, or the God of deserts? To which to go?" The book is in the Harvard College Library.
[11] *Pierre*, p. 125.

In *Pierre* the element of isolation from the world, a part of the Ishmael character, appears most strongly. The angel who gave Hagar the name for Ishmael before his birth also prophesied his nature: "And he will be a wild man; his hand will be against every man, and every man's hand against him; and he shall dwell in the presence of all his brethren."[12] To a greater degree than any other hero of Melville's, Pierre is such a wild man, or wild ass of a man, as a literal translation has it. His contemporaries regard him as insane. He is opposed at one time or another to his mother, his father's spirit, his betrothed, his publishers, his public, his kinsmen—even to Isabel, toward whom his attitude becomes divided. In the end his hand is literally against Glendinning Stanly and Frederick Tartan, and their hands are against him: when Glen lashes him with a cowhide, Pierre draws pistols and slays them both.

Israel Potter is one more manifestation of the Ishmael character, although, as in *White Jacket,* the original Old Testament story is not actually cited. Perhaps Potter's name, which he found in his source, determined Melville's procedure here. At any rate, once again the name of Ishmael is exchanged for another Biblical name, while the character type remains the same. Potter is Israel, and his story follows the story of the Hebrew tribes in their forty years of exile. The parallel is more carefully carried out than most of Melville's parallels, and at the same time it is less ingenious and provocative.

The extent of the analogy is particularly noticeable when the novel is compared with its source: *The Life and Remarkable Adventures of Israel R. Potter.* Here is the Scriptural name of the hero and the account of his life of exile, but there is no mention of the Hebrews. There is, in fact,

[12] Gen. 16:12. When Pierre's grandfather is likened to Abraham, the allusion is to Abraham the patriarch, not the father of Ishmael (*Pierre,* p. 40).

only one allusion to the Bible. In Melville's version seven references develop the allegory inherent in Potter's name and fate, and twenty more deepen the Biblical tone of the whole. The first of them is prelusive. Whereas Potter begins with the testimony, "I was born of reputable parents,"[13] Melville calls these parents good Puritans who, like the mother of Captain Ahab, prophetically named him, "since, for more than forty years, poor Potter wandered in the wild wilderness of the world's extremest hardships and ills."[14]

This figure of a wilderness to describe a city—the same which in *Pierre* is fleetingly associated with the desert experience of Hagar and Ishmael—recurs in *Israel Potter*. And although in this novel the hero is not engaged in a search for the ultimate, the image is still Biblical. After escaping from Falmouth, Potter continues his way toward London, a journey described in the title of the twenty-second chapter: "Something Further of Ethan Allen; With Israel's Flight toward the Wilderness." The next two chapters, entitled "Israel in Egypt," relate how he finds employment in a brickyard outside London. "Poor Israel!" exclaimed his narrator, "well named—bondsman in the English Egypt."[15] At the end of thirteen weeks he proceeds to London, where his adventures, telescoped into a few paragraphs, continue to parallel those of the Hebrews:

For the most part, what befell Israel during his forty years' wanderings in the London deserts, surpassed the forty years in the natural wilderness of the outcast Hebrews under Moses.

In that London fog, went before him the ever-present cloud by day, but no pillar of fire by the night. . . .[16]

In his last days Potter finds comfort in telling his one surviving child of "the far Canaan beyond the sea"[17]—New

[13] *Magazine of History*, Extra No. 16 (New York, 1911) p. 621. (A reprint.)

[14] *Israel Potter*, p. 5.   [15] *Ibid.*, p. 209.

[16] *Ibid.*, p. 214.   [17] *Ibid.*, p. 221.

England. And the tale ends when the old man, like the tribes themselves, returns to the land from which he originally set out.

The allegory in *Israel Potter* is perhaps too obvious to be artistic. Moreover, the effect of his specific allusions to the Hebrew wanderings is often weakened by Melville's supplementary Biblical references when they might have been supported. By carelessly calling Potter's child "the spared Benjamin of his old age,"[18] he confused Israel the man and Israel the nation. He exceeded the time boundary of the original story and leapt eight hundred years to the Babylonian captivity when he said that Potter observed, in 1793, "the exodus of the lost tribes of soldiers."[19] The title of Chapter V, "Israel in the Lion's Den," is a mixed metaphor. Even his chapter headings, alluding first to the Hebrews' flight to the wilderness and then to their sojourn in Egypt, reverse the original order of events.

That Melville should be so inattentive to his Biblical details in a novel which is, on the other hand, the result of decided attention to realistic detail seems strange. But the lapse bears out one of the chief characterizations of his Scriptural allusions: they are most effective when they illumine the mystery of some deep, interior experience. Such experience, for all the excellence of its Franklin character and its battle scenes, *Israel Potter* does not pretend to picture.

Twice more does the character of Ishmael, the social outcast, enter Melville's pages, though not to be completely drawn. Pitch and Ungar are also Ishmaels. In *The Confidence-Man: His Masquerade,* where there is more than one masquerade, the trappings of Pitch, the Missouri bachelor, are among the more easily recognized. He wears a bearskin coat and a coonskin hat, and carries a double-barreled gun. In the three dialogues between him and the Cosmopolitan he reveals his attitude to nature, individuals, and

[18] *Ibid.*   [19] *Ibid.*, p. 217.

society. All, he is convinced, are evil. In short, his disguise is that of an Ishmael, as the Cosmopolitan perceives: " 'To you, an Ishmael, disguising in sportiveness my intent, I came ambassador from the human race, charged with the assurance that for your mislike they bore no answering grudge, but sought to conciliate accord between you and them.' "[20]

In view of the thorough irony of *The Confidence-Man,* Pitch is perhaps of all Melville's Ishmaels the one who best reveals his deep sympathy with this character. Toward it he is never unsympathetic, but he never seems so serious as here. Such bitterness as Pitch's in another context might appear to be a mood, like one of the sailor Ishmael's, or a *weltanschauung,* such as those Babbalanja delighted to analyze and compare. But on board the *Fidèle* the nature of everything is belied by its appearance. Here Pitch's hatred is true love, just as the heart of the Indian-killing Colonel Moredock is kind. So tight is Melville's logic that even the reverse of the paradox is true: to love men is actually to hate them. The first city, Pitch reminds the Cosmopolitan, was built by the first murderer, Cain; for only criminals, he declares, fear solitude.

With the episode of Moredock, of whom Noble is reminded by Pitch, the scriptural image of the wilderness occurs again. The typical backwoodsman, according to Noble, is a lonely, solitary character, " 'Worthy to be compared with Moses in the Exodus.' "[21] And this time the figure is deliberately chosen for its religious significance. For Moredock, according to Noble's story,

" 'was not unaware that to be a consistent Indian-hater involves the renunciation of ambition, with its objects—the pomps and glories of the world; and since religion, pronouncing such things vanities, accounts it merit to renounce them, therefore,

[20] *The Confidence-Man,* p. 185. [21] *Ibid.,* p. 194.

so far as this goes, Indian-hating, whatever may be thought of it in other respects, may be regarded as not wholly without the efficacy of a devout sentiment.' "[22]

The Indian-hating interlude in *The Confidence-Man*, which is in fact the crux of the book, thus places two of Melville's symbols in curious juxtaposition. Elsewhere in this novel, as in others, Melville used Indian culture to represent primitive innocence, as he also used the culture of the Polynesians, the fable of Eden, and the idealism of the Gospels. And elsewhere this state though immature is idyllic, outgrown but loved and longed for. That it is here a state to be fiercely and implacably warred upon is not, however, a contradiction of thought, but an ironic presentation of precisely the same symbolic value. This is the cruel farewell taken by the tragically committed Pierre of the fair Lucy, by Hamlet of Ophelia.

And since the true frontiersman must thus hate and kill Indians, who though innocent are no more harmless than the panther or the leviathan, it is appropriate that the setting for the feud is the wilderness, the symbolic scene of mature experience throughout Melville. One of the changes, in fact, which he made in Judge Hall's narrative, which he often quoted verbatim, was to say that Moredock's mother wandered not "from one territory to another," but "from wilderness to wilderness, always on the frontier."[23]

For the inhabitant of this wilderness, Colonel Moredock, is the type of Melville's unwearying seeker of truth, a deep-sea denizen, a Moses. He, too, may be called an Ishmael, and, like Pitch's, his exile is voluntary. The fact is significant. Melville's early Ishmaels—Redburn, White Jacket,

[22] *Ibid.*, p. 208.

[23] James Hall, *Sketches of History, Life, and Manners in the West* (Philadelphia, 1835), II, 79. Quoted in Elizabeth Foster, "Herman Melville's *The Confidence-Man*: Its Origins and Meaning" (doctoral dissertation, Yale University, 1942). Miss Foster was first to establish this passage in Hall as the source of Melville's Indian-hating episode.

Ishmael of the *Pequod,* and Pierre—are thrust into the role
by a fate beyond their control. But his last two, Pitch and
Ungar, choose to be outcasts. The character becomes increasingly philosophic and less dramatic. Above all, it becomes far more than the character of a simple misanthrope,
as its creator considered the necessity of solitude to salvation.

Such a necessity can but have been distressing to Melville the democrat and the humanist, and the isolation
which he gradually insisted upon for the earnest thinker
was entered not in hatred but in sorrow. Nor was it a
tenet he found in a single source. Increasingly in the books
he read he marked passages dealing with the loneliness of
genius, the gulf between an author and his public, the melancholy attending true aspiration. To Schopenhauer's conception of the artist—a man destined by his sharper per-
ceptions and his greater conquests of will to suffer isolation from his contemporaries—he gave his aged assent, and
thus came near to joining the thematic progression through
Nietzsche and Wagner to Mann.

Yet the Biblical imagery persists, indeed is most obvious
of all in *Clarel.* Here, it is true, all the characters are Ishmaels of a sort, for all have forsaken society to dwell temporarily in the desert. Among them Mortmain, Ungar, and
Nathan have most in common with the Biblical character,
and Ungar is figuratively associated with him. In the
scheme of the poem this "wandering Ishmael from the
West"[24] replaces Mortmain, an even more bitter critic of
society and like Ishmael illegitimate, who dies halfway
through the narrative.

Ungar merits the comparison with Ishmael well enough,
having alienated his Southern compatriots by opposing
slavery and the victors of the Civil War by renouncing
their spoils. A descendant of the colonial Tilly and an Indian maid, he has "An Anglo brain, but Indian heart,"

[24] *Clarel,* II, 199.

"forest eyes," and a "forest name"[25]—which, incidentally, is German for "raw" or "unseasoned." It is a background agreeing with that of Melville's other primitives—Polynesians, Greeks, inhabitants of Eden—whose idyllic life in nature must eventually be succeeded by harsh experience.

At this point, in fact, Ungar's background blends with that of Nathan, whose father is buried near the Illinois Indian mounds, and who, because he has forsaken more that was dear to him in migrating to Palestine, is closer to Melville's Ishmael type than Ungar. The brief sketch of Nathan, indeed, abounds in some of Melville's favorite symbols. He is haunted by two white apparitions, both suggestive of death: the skull near his father's grave, entwined with flowers, and the landslide of the White Hills, which killed his uncle. His landlocked home seems to promise only destruction. Glimpsing a wider scene first upon reading the Scot's book on deism, he thereafter tills his soil like Adam did after tasting of knowledge:

> When thrust from Eden out to dearth
> And blest no more, and wise in shame.[26]

From his own Eden, Nathan is finally led by the Jewess Agar, whom significantly he meets in a lake port and who converts him to Judaism. Leaving behind him "fair fields and household charms,"[27] he sets out with her for Palestine.

Agar's name itself clarifies the Ishmael pattern of Nathan's life. For while his own name is that of David's prophet who helped foil Adonijah's conspiracy—a story marked in Melville's Bible and alluded to in *Clarel*—it does not accord in any unusual way with his character. Agar, however, bears the name of the Arabian tribes which are also called Hagarenes or Hagrites and which were traditionally supposed to be the descendants of Hagar, like the

[25] *Ibid.*, II, 179, 161.
[26] *Ibid.*, I, 73.
[27] *Ibid.*, I, 77.

Ishmaelites. Both Hagarenes and Ishmaelites are words Melville underscored in his Bible and groups he referred to as inhabiting the desert in *Clarel*.

And this time Melville's desert is literal. Nathan, Ungar, Clarel, and the other pilgrims traverse the dry land of Palestine in the hope of discovering some vestige of the divinity which once lived there. It is true, on the one hand, that the scene of their journey may be taken as an image of Melville's contemporary world, parched and faithless. But it is not only that. Again a wasteland—of rationalism, of doubt, of scientific disbelief—must be visited if the riddle of existence is at all to be solved.

Hence the contrast with this barren scene is effected not so much by the glimpses of palms and grass growing in its midst as by "The contrast of their vernal homes";[28] by the memory of green lands far away which the pilgrims have forsaken in order to undertake their pilgrimage: Illinois, Rhode Island, the isles of the southern sea. Rolfe recalls an idyllic episode of his seafaring youth when he escaped from his ship to live for a while with a Polynesian tribe:

> "Where Eden, isled, empurpled glows
> In old Mendanna's sea. . . ."[29]

His nostalgia is like Bulkington's for the lee shore or Pierre's for Saddle Meadows, which nevertheless he must renounce if he would explore the boundless universe.

It is also like Adam's yearning for Eden, an image which in *Clarel* Melville superimposed on the image of the revelation in the wilderness. Nathan is like another outcast Adam. Vine enjoins the palm to win the desert " 'To dreams of Eden,' "[30] and Rolfe compares the same tree to " 'Adam's flight Without compulsion or the sin.' "[31] Clarel's courtship

---

[28] *Ibid.*, II, 21.
[30] *Ibid.*, II, 127.
[29] *Ibid.*, II, 140.
[31] *Ibid.*, II, 141.

of Ruth, when in fancy they roam "green uplands free," "Wins Eden back" and makes the desert and the man who was crucified there seem "foreign—forged—incongruous."[32]

One other character in *Clarel* not only seems to have an Old Testament antecedent but bears his name as well: Nehemiah. The native of Narragansett Bay, whom Clarel meets in Jerusalem, has come there to help usher in the promised millennium. While Nathan, who is his obvious foil, would rebuild Palestine for the Jews, Nehemiah regards them as forerunners of the true Christian faith. Fondly he believes the prophecy:

> Zion restore, convert the Jew,
> Reseat him here, the waste bedew;
> Then Christ returneth: so it ran.[33]

Connected with no church or mission, Nehemiah devotes himself simply to distributing tracts, each of which he is convinced

> "points the way,
> Sole way, dear heart, whereby ye may
> Rebuild the Temple."[34]

He is a poor figure indeed beside the proud Jewish patriot of the fifth century B.C., yet this Nehemiah is reminiscent of that one. For Nehemiah the prophet, learning while he was cupbearer at the court of Artaxerxes of the ruined state of Jerusalem, had himself appointed governor of Judea in order that he might rebuild the city walls. He, too, left his home for Zion, there to restore her. The story, not referred to elsewhere in Melville's books, bears marks in his Bible.

---

[32] *Ibid.*, I, 110. W. E. Sedgwick seems to think Melville renounced the innocent life of natural man even as early as *Typee* (*Herman Melville*, Cambridge, 1944).

[33] *Clarel*, I, 34-35.

[34] *Ibid.*, I, 67.

II

In addition to furnishing Melville with the original Ishmael the Old Testament gave him also a model for his most celebrated character: Captain Ahab, who is named for King Ahab, seventh king of Israel after the division of the tribes.[35] In fact, King Ahab's story and that of his predecessor, King Jeroboam, account for an entire group of persons in *Moby-Dick*: Ahab, Fedallah, Starbuck, Elijah, Gabriel, Macey, and the *Jeroboam* and the *Rachel*.

The *Pequod's* Captain Ahab is associated with his Biblical namesake at the outset of the narrative. Acquainting Ishmael with his history, Peleg reminds the young sailor that " 'Ahab of old, thou knowest, was a crowned king!' " To this the Presbyterian Ishmael replies: " 'And a very vile one. When that wicked king was slain, the dogs, did they not lick his blood?' "[36] Whereupon, begging him never to repeat this remark, Peleg relates the circumstances of Ahab's being so named and the predictions which have followed him:

"Captain Ahab did not name himself. 'Twas a foolish, ignorant whim of his crazy, widowed mother, who died when he was only a twelvemonth old. And yet the old squaw Tistig, at Gay Head, said that the name would somehow prove prophetic. And, perhaps, other fools like her may tell thee the same. I wish to warn thee. It's a lie."[37]

Despite Peleg's valiant protest, the prophecy about Captain Ahab does not prove to be a lie. Not only the tragic end of his life but the essential duality of his character also is foreshadowed in the Old Testament story. For the pic-

[35] This, of course, does not preclude the possibility that Melville got the name of Ahab from another source and then developed the Biblical analogy, as he did in *Israel Potter*. In J. Ross Browne's *Etchings of a Whaling Cruise* "Captain A———" of the *Styx* bears a distinct resemblance to Captain Ahab of the *Pequod* (Anderson, *op. cit.*, p. 43).

[36] *Moby-Dick*, I, 99.

[37] *Ibid.*, I, 100.

ture of King Ahab which emerges in I Kings is a composite of two points of view: that of the sources, according to which he was an able and energetic ruler, and that of the didactic compiler, who saw him also as a dangerous innovator and a patron of foreign gods.

King Ahab's political shrewdness is evident in the series of alliances he made with surrounding kingdoms, his accruing wealth in the ivory palace he built. He married the princess Jezebel of Phoenicia, made peace with Jehoshaphat of Judah, and, according to Assyrian inscriptions, furnished Ben-hadad of Damascus with troops against Assyria. Being in his turn attacked by Ben-hadad, he concluded his victory by sparing his enemy's life and arranging for each kingdom to have bazaars in the capital of the other. The alliance was thus one of trade and commerce, and as such was violently opposed by the prophetic party of Israel. It lasted, according to the Biblical record, only three years. When hostilities with Damascus were renewed, Ahab was slain in battle, defending his kingdom. It was then that the dogs, as Ishmael ghoulishly remembered, licked his blood.

Like the king of Israel, the captain of the *Pequod* is shrewd in his secular associations. As a captain he is able and courageous; as a whaleman he is successful, for forty years temporizing with the great dangers of the deep for the wealth which it yields. The very evidence of this success is fantastically like that in King Ahab's story: Captain Ahab, too, lives in an ivory house, "the ivory *Pequod*" as it is often called, tricked out in trophies of whale bones and teeth from profitable voyages. Yet in the end trade is no less treacherous to the captain than to the king. Perhaps it could not be otherwise. For as Ishmael's account testifies, its nature is to be now a friend and now an enemy, and the best merchants are, like Bildad and Starbuck, strictly utilitarian. To this category Ahab apparently belonged until his last voyage, which, incidentally, was to have taken three years, just the length of time which King Ahab's bazaars in Damascus lasted. But the *Pequod's* last voyage, unlike its others, is not entirely commercial, and the blame for its disaster must be divided. From the morning on which Captain Ahab nails up the golden doubloon as a prize for Moby-Dick, it becomes a pursuit through invisible waters of an immortal spirit. And a duel is begun between the prudent Starbuck and the haunted Ahab. For Ahab cannot compromise. In the realm in which he hunts the white whale there are no alliances with the enemy. His voyage is disastrous when, in the midst of a profitable whale hunt, he becomes involved in the unequivocal pursuit of supernatural truth.

All this recalls the second nature of King Ahab, an able politician but in the religious sphere a patron of foreign gods. It is on this account that Ishmael remembers him as "vile" and "wicked." In the Biblical narrative Ahab offended Jehovah by introducing the Phoenician Baal as one of the gods of Israel at the time he married Jezebel of Phoenicia, whose father, according to Josephus, was a priest of Astarte. It appears that Ahab never intended thus to displace but only to supplement Jehovah. But Jehovah, who claimed the exclusive right to Israel's worship, tolerated no alliances with neighboring gods, or even with neighboring kings. He never forgave Ahab for sparing Ben-hadad's life. With Jehovah an enemy was always an enemy. And so he contrived with false prophets to bring King Ahab to destruction. Like the captain of the *Pequod,* King Ahab attempted to compromise in an uncompromising realm.

Indeed, Peleg's epithet for Captain Ahab is perhaps a better description of King Ahab than any in the Book of Kings: " 'a grand, ungodly, god-like man.' "[38] Like King Ahab, he worships pagan gods. His particular deity is the

[38] *Ibid.,* I, 99.

spirit of fire, and he adores other objects of this cult: the light, the sun, the stars. His harpooner is a fire-worshiping Zoroastrian, Fedallah, the Parsee. In the midst of the typhoon Ahab invokes the fire already burning at the mast-ends, whereupon it leaps thrice its height—a feat itself which is a match for Elijah's calling down the fire on Mount Carmel to confound King Ahab's Baalite prophets. Finally, as though all this were not "ungodly" enough, Captain Ahab tempers the whale barbs not in water but in the heathen blood of Tashtego, Queequeg, and Daggoo. His voice is lifted defiantly to heaven, in what Melville told Hawthorne was the very motto of the book: "'Ego non baptizo te in nomine patris, sed in nomine diaboli!'"[39]

Of course, Ahab's death is not an instance of divine retribution in the orthodox sense. A romantic paganism is part of his nature, and not the least element of which he is compounded is Milton's Satan himself. The epithets applied to him by Ishmael and Starbuck—"infidel," "impious," "diabolic," "blasphemous"—describe a towering rebel who is akin to all other rebels in history, King Ahab among them.

Yet when in this character Captain Ahab does meet death, it is through hearkening, like King Ahab, to false prophecy. In the case of King Ahab it was the jealous Jehovah who betrayed him. Before trying to recover Ramoth-Gilead, which was in the hands of his old enemy, the King of Damascus, Ahab consulted his four hundred prophets. They promised him victory. But Micaiah, "a prophet of the Lord," who was summoned at the request of Ahab's ally, Jehoshaphat, said he would be slain. To explain this discrepancy in the two prophecies, Micaiah then related a vision he had, in which Ahab's prophets were revealed to be divinely inspired liars. On this occasion he saw Jehovah enthroned and surrounded by angels, and heard him

[39] *Ibid.*, II, 261.

call for someone who would persuade Ahab to engage in the fatal battle. For Ahab's death had apparently already been determined, and to the divine inquiry a spirit appeared who said: "I will go forth, and I will be a lying spirit in the mouth of all his prophets."[40] But in spite of Micaiah's story, Ahab believed the words of the false prophets, and thus deluded went to his death.

A false prophet contributes also to Captain Ahab's death. He is Fedallah, who appears increasingly in this role in the last of *Moby-Dick*. His actual prophecy, however, sounds less like an echo of the Bible than of *Macbeth,* with Birnam Wood moving to Dunsinane. Cryptically Fedallah predicts that before Ahab dies he must see two hearses on the sea—the first not made by mortal hands, the second made of American wood. He promises even then to precede his captain as pilot, and concludes by assuring Ahab that only hemp can kill him. All this is an accurate forecast of the tragic end, but it fatally deceives Ahab, who sees in it an assurance of victory.

On the other hand, there is no end to the honest prophecies that are made to Captain Ahab. The balance of influence is reversed in the two stories. King Ahab had four hundred false prophets and one who was true, but Melville sees to it, with characteristic irony, that Captain Ahab defies all creation in order to believe his single malevolent angel. The pleadings of Starbuck, the ravings of the mad Gabriel, the testimony of ships which have met the whale, the whisperings of his own heart, and a host of omens in nature— all these he ignores, heeding only Fedallah.

Starbuck, in the intimate relation he bears to his captain, also has an antecedent in the original Ahab story. With his frenzied attempts to conciliate the powers which Ahab is determined to alienate he suggests the God-fearing Obadiah, governor of King Ahab's house, who, when Jezebel

[40] I Kings 22:22.

persecuted the Israelite prophets, concealed a hundred of them in a cave and sustained them there until the danger was past. He was on good terms, too, with the prophet Elijah.

This prophet, the great Tishbite who denounced King Ahab and Queen Jezebel, provided Melville with the name for the pock-marked lunatic whom Ishmael and Queequeg encounter twice before sailing. As the two avidly listen, he enumerates the strange tales which have been told about Captain Ahab and insinuates that not only he but the entire crew of the *Pequod* will never return from the voyage. The significance of his name can hardly have escaped the Biblically astute Ishmael, who calls him a "prophet" and exclaims portentously as they leave the creature, "Elijah!"

Possibly Ishmael remembered that the actual words of the prophet Elijah to King Ahab include a curse, which in the Books of Kings is habitually pronounced upon the wicked kings of Israel: "[I] will make thine house like the house of Jeroboam the son of Nebat."[41] Its meaning is devastatingly clear. Jeroboam, the first king of Israel after the tribal division, though actually a courageous opponent of the tyrant Solomon, is charged in the Old Testament with fostering sacrilegious rituals and sacrifices in the new kingdom. For his offense Jehovah allowed his son to die and vowed to destroy his dynasty. And so the wicked successors of Jeroboam were described as walking "in all the way of Jeroboam the son of Nebat, and in his sin wherewith he made Israel to sin,"[42] and were promised the same punishment. Jeroboam is thus not only a forerunner, but his fate is a forecast of the fates of all the kings who followed him, including King Ahab.

And for this predecessor of King Ahab the *Jeroboam* in *Moby-Dick*, a predecessor of the *Pequod*, is named. Of the four vessels met by the *Pequod* which have already en-

[41] *Ibid.*, 21:22, *et passim*.   [42] *Ibid.*, 16:26, *et passim*.

countered Ahab's quarry, the *Jeroboam* is the first. Her fate is prophetic. It is a message of warning to all who follow, articulated by Gabriel and vindicated by the *Samuel Enderby,* the *Rachel,* the *Delight,* and at last the *Pequod.* The *Jeroboam's* pursuit of Moby-Dick has resulted in the loss of her mate and may in some mysterious way be responsible for the epidemic among her crew, but the whale has escaped. And so the other four vessels, pursuing the same course, meet similar misfortunes, without slaying Moby-Dick.

The "utter wreck" of the *Pequod,* in its turn, was probably made inevitable by Melville's own flair for spectacle, but the corroboration for it is complete in the stories of King Jeroboam and King Ahab. Compared with the partial losses of the *Jeroboam,* the *Enderby,* the *Rachel,* and the *Delight,* the destruction of the *Pequod* is appalling indeed. But it is a fitting end for the monomania of Ahab, which none of the other captains shared. So in the case of King Ahab the account of his death is elaborated by more details of violence than are to be found in that of any of the Israelite kings before him. The reason is not far to seek. He vexed Jehovah more than all the rest: ". . . and Ahab did more to provoke the Lord God of Israel to anger than all the kings of Israel that were before him."[43]

Without doubt, the seventh king of Israel was a memorable man. Melville did not soon forget him. When in *Clarel* he cast about for a figure to describe the appearance of two of the pilgrims, Mortmain and Rolfe, he found it in the story he had used long before.

> Mortmain aloof and single sat—
> In range with Rolfe, as viewed from mat
> Where Vine reposed, observing there
> That these in contour of the head
> And goodly profile made a pair,

[43] *Ibid.,* 16:33.

> Though one looked like a statue dead.
> Methinks (mused Vine), 'tis Ahab's court
> And yon the Tishbite; he'll consort
> Not long, but Kedron [*sic*] seek.[44]

Ahab's prophet, too, lingered in his memory, recalled by the surly Mortmain, "the Gileadite In Obadiah's way."[45] A wise man was still solitary, still an inhabitant of the desert.

Now the history of King Jeroboam, part of the background history of King Ahab, is memorialized in *Moby-Dick* by more than the name of a vessel. In the crew of the *Jeroboam* there are two characters who correspond to members of King Jeroboam's household: Macey and Gabriel. The mate Macey, who is dexterously lifted from the boat by the whale and cast to his death in the sea, takes the place of King Jeroboam's son, Abijah. When Abijah fell ill his parents appealed in vain to Jehovah's prophet; the child died for the father's sins.

The role of this prophet, Ahijah, is matched aboard the *Jeroboam* by Gabriel. At first assuring King Jeroboam of success, Ahijah was compelled by the king's idolatry to condemn not only his son but his whole house to death. Gabriel of the *Jeroboam* was also a prophet, so called among the Neskyeuna Shakers, and his predictions to Macey and to Ahab are fulfilled. His argument with Macey, whom he tries to dissuade from lowering for Moby-Dick, is similar to Ahijah's quarrel with the idolatrous King Jeroboam: Macey is committing sacrilege in hunting Moby-Dick, since the whale is an incarnation of the Shaker deity.

But of course, unlike Ahijah, Gabriel is mad. And to emphasize the fact Melville associated him thoroughly with apocalyptic lore, almost obliterating his connection with the Jeroboam story. In calling himself the Archangel Gabriel,

[44] *Clarel*, II, 55-56.
[45] *Ibid.*, II, 150. See also I, 313, where Mortmain is associated with the brook Cherith, beside which Elijah lived.

this character assumes the name of the being sent to reveal to Daniel the meaning of his vision, though not identified as an archangel until the New Testament. Otherwise, however, Melville's Gabriel is more imbued with the vision of John; he carries in his vest pocket the seventh vial of God's wrath—the earthquake—and announces himself deliverer and vicar-general of the isles of the sea. In this scheme the fate of Macey has an explanation quite different from its meaning in relation to the story of King Jeroboam. His death is the result of the wrath of God being poured out of one of the vials, as Gabriel says. And the ensuing epidemic on board the *Jeroboam* may be attributed to the same cause. For the angels with the vials are, in the Evangelist's vision, the same angels who have the seven last plagues, and the plagues seem to be visited on the earth by means of the vials' being broken.

But there is an important limitation to this dire program in Revelation. The vials and the plagues are to destroy only the heathen world, or those who worship the beast with seven heads. This suggests the analogous fact that in *Moby-Dick* only those who pursue the white whale are doomed. It suggests, further, that Melville had identified in his imagination the whale and the beast which "[did] rise up out of the sea"[46] to overcome its virtuous opponent and even to curse God. Such an identification is never expressed, but it would account for the name which he gave his Neskyeuna Shaker. For although this name is not part of the story of the seven vials at all, there is a connection between the two. The beast in Revelation, with its leopard, bear, and lion members and its ten horns, is a combination of the four beasts which rise from the sea in Daniel's vision, to be explained by the angelic Gabriel. Thus linked by the beast or beasts of the sea, the name and the message of the *Jeroboam's* "prophet" are naturally, even inevitably, related.

[46] Rev. 13:1; see also Dan. 7:3.

It is true that in Melville's mind, as in the mind of Coleridge, many associations existed whose links are not visible in what he wrote. The name of Gabriel points to one of these associations. The names of the ships in *Moby-Dick* indicate another. Though two Israelite kings—Ahab and Jeroboam—are the only ones whose names appear prominently in the novel, others were in Melville's thought. His imagery attests the fact. It seems even possible that his recollection of the entire succession determined the number of ships in the novel. Beginning with the *Pequod,* excluding the *Moss* with its short run from New Bedford to Nantucket, and ending with the *Delight* there are ten vessels which sail the open sea. The number is equal to the number of kings of Israel from Saul, the first, to Ahab. In this series the *Jeroboam* comes fourth, corresponding to the place of King Jeroboam I.

Nor were Jeroboam and Ahab the only wicked ones among them. A long line of wicked rulers at last drew Jehovah's wrath upon the entire kingdom, and the Babylonian captivity ensued. This sequel to the Ahab story is briefly touched upon at the conclusion of *Moby-Dick* in the name of the whaler *Rachel.* Cruising deviously over the waters in search of the captain's son, who was lost in pursuit of the white whale, this vessel is pictured as a mother inconsolable in the loss of her children: "But by her still halting course and winding, woeful way, you plainly saw that this ship that so wept with spray still remained without comfort. She was Rachel, weeping for her children, because they were not."[47]

She personifies Jacob's wife, the spiritual mother of all Israel, whom Jeremiah imagines weeping over the captivity of the remnants of her nation, as on their way to Babylon they pass near her tomb. This is the ship which in the end rescues Ishmael, the *Pequod's* sole survivor. So in Jere-

[47] *Moby-Dick,* II, 315.

miah's prophecy Rachel is comforted by the assurance of Jehovah that, despite the sins of their sovereigns for which they have had to suffer, the tribes will be returned from captivity.

There is, in any case, a decided association in Melville's mind between the ships in *Moby-Dick* and characters in the Bible, evidence again of his fondness for personification. There is the *Jeroboam,* the *Pequod* captained by Ahab, the *Rachel,* and the *Jungfrau.* Unlike the other three, however, this last ship is not a piece of Israelite history. It represents the Five Foolish Virgins of Jesus's parable, who, going to meet the Bridegroom without oil in their lamps, tried to borrow from their five wise sisters. For Master Derick de Deer of the *Jungfrau,* or *Virgin* as Ishmael obligingly translates, eagerly boards the *Pequod* to obtain oil from Ahab for his empty lamp-feeder.

There is one more character in *Moby-Dick* who seems to be named for a character in the Bible. He is the Quaker Captain Bildad, half-owner of the *Pequod.* In contrast to his profane partner, Captain Peleg—whose name is also Biblical—he is pious, poring over the Scriptures and interspersing his nautical vernacular with quotations from them. But he also has a reputation for being a hard master and has devoted his life to the spilling of whale blood. His name is appropriate to his type, for it is the name of Bildad the Shuhite, the "traditionalist" of Job's three friends. Actually, the speeches of the three are scarcely individualized in the poem, and a wisdom philosophy is common to all: only the wicked are punished and the righteous shall surely prosper. This thesis, strenuously denied by Job and by the author of *Moby-Dick,* underlies Captain Bildad's prudent advice to the sailors: "'Don't whale it too much a Lord's days, men; but don't miss a fair chance either, that's rejecting Heaven's good gifts.'"[48]

[48] *Ibid.,* I, 130.

Bildad the proprietor, like Bildad the Shuhite, has perhaps not divorced religion and business, as Ishmael thought, but united them. He seems to practice piety and to aim at the conversion of all his sailors in order to insure a prosperous voyage for the *Pequod*. The verse of Scripture in which he is engrossed when Ishmael meets him affords Melville singular opportunity for punning upon Ishmael's "lay" in the ship's profits, but at the same time it is one of the few New Testament maxims which matches the utilitarianism of Job's friends, with its cunning advice about spiritual dividends: "'*Lay* not up for yourselves treasures upon earth, where moth—'"[49]

III

In the characterization of two of his titanic heroes, Pierre and Billy Budd, Melville drew upon a New Testament figure: Jesus. The relationship between model and creation, however, is far more tenuous than it is in the case of his Ishmaels and his Ahab, since this time both model and creation are more complex. They touch at but a single point. Like Jesus, Pierre embodies unselfish devotion to an ethical cause, and Billy Budd represents innocence crucified by law.

In these narratives, it is true, both central character and theme have a Biblical cast, and the two often seem to be one. In *Billy Budd,* where conflicting qualities of good and evil are personified, they are virtually indistinguishable. Therefore, while Budd, Claggart, and Vere correspond in general to Jesus, Judas, and God in the Crucifixion story, they do so as symbols rather than as personalities and are thus aspects of Melville's themes rather than of his characterization.

In *Pierre,* however, there is a distinction between Biblical theme and character. While the theme is ostensibly the

⁴⁹ *Ibid.,* I, 96.

practicality of the Gospel ethics, the similarity between Pierre and Jesus is not altogether their practice of these precepts. It is essentially their unswerving allegiance to destiny. This passion, of course, moves all Melville's major characters, constituting their kinship with the Marlovian rather than the Shakespearean hero. But in Pierre alone it is described with reference to Jesus.

Three brief scenes are devoted to the analogy. For though he is pictured as nurtured from birth in the Christian tradition, the Glendinning scion is not at once associated with the founder of that tradition. Only with his decision to abandon Lucy and marry Isabel does he penetrate the superficialities of Christianity; only his nobility, his obedience to the god within him, prompts him to such unprofitable action: "Thus, in the Enthusiast to Duty, the heaven-begotten Christ is born; and will not own a mortal parent, and spurns and rends all mortal bonds."[50] And having made his decision without even seeing Isabel, Pierre prepares the next morning for their first meeting with the prayer: "May heaven new-string my soul, and confirm me in the Christ-like feeling I first felt."[51] On the occasion of their second meeting he is again likened to Jesus, as he compares their simple meal of bread and water to the Last Supper: " 'Give me the cup; hand it me with thine own hand. So:—Isabel, my heart and soul are now full of deepest reverence; yet I do dare to call this the real sacrament of the supper.—Eat with me.' "[52]

At greater length Pierre plays the role of Jesus among the priests and elders in his argument with the Reverend Mr. Falsgrave at the breakfast table. When the subject of the wayward Delly is introduced, Falsgrave quotes the Mosaic law: " ' "The sins of the father shall be visited upon

[50] *Pierre*, p. 149.
[51] *Ibid.*, pp. 149-150.
[52] *Ibid.*, p. 228.

the children to the third generation. . . ." ' "⁵³ In fact, throughout the scene Falsgrave, though a minister of the Gospel, upholds rather the legalism of the Old Testament. His brooch, from which the napkin drops at appropriate intervals, displays the figures of the serpent and the dove, constituting an allegory more characteristic of the wisdom books than of the Gospels. It was, indeed, a favorite symbol of wisdom with Melville, who cited it in describing such diverse characters as Benjamin Franklin and Billy Budd.

Pierre, on the other hand, responds to Falsgrave by citing the story of the woman taken in adultery. Needless to say, his attitude toward Delly is the same as Jesus's there. Furthermore, the same authority, expounded by a professional religious, confronts Pierre as it confronted Jesus: the Mosaic law. For Falsgrave quotes it, though inaccurately, and the story of the adulteress in the New Testament account is introduced by the scribes' interrogation of Jesus regarding the same ancient code: "Now Moses in the law commanded us, that such should be stoned: but what sayest thou?"⁵⁴

Once his course of action has been determined, the Biblical allusions which associate Pierre with Jesus disappear from his story. It is in forming his decision that he is most like the founder of Christianity; in renouncing the world; in disputing the law. Once his fearless and fatal position has been chosen, he becomes merely a young idealist striving to obey what he remembers of the Sermon on the Mount, one of the followers whom Plinlimmon's pamphlet sharply distinguishes from the leader. And once it becomes apparent that his lot, like theirs, will be tragic,

---

⁵³ *Ibid.*, p. 140. This is no exact quotation of any verse in the Old Testament, where almost the same words are to be found in several places; see Exod. 20:5, 34:7; Num. 14:18; Deut. 5:9.

⁵⁴ John 8:5. Melville checked John 8:7, 8, 11 in his copy of the New Testament and owned also a print depicting this scene (Braswell, *op. cit.*, p. 79).

even the theme of the Gospel ethics is dropped. After Pierre's arrival in the city it is broached no more. Its purpose is the motivation of action which itself has no religious character and which moves to no religious end.

Pierre, Billy Budd, and the dozen or more other characters whom Melville seems to have drawn substantially from Old and New Testament originals are not, of course, the only ones he described by means of allusions to the Bible, and indeed to many other literary sources. Numerous briefer analogues are among the figures of speech which crowd his pages. It was one of his favorite methods of description. Thus, Billy Budd is pictured not only as Jesus, but as Adam and Isaac as well. Pierre is like Esau selling his birthright; he also sees himself in a dream as Enceladus, the mutilated Titan, and recognized similarities between his life and Hamlet's. Ahab is said to be Adam under the weight of the centuries, Cellini's statue of Perseus, Tamburlaine, a Greek god, a Persian fire-worshiper. In a single scene Moby-Dick is likened to Jupiter the bull eloping with Europa, to Antiochus's elephants, and also to the natural bridge in Virginia.

By this device of brief analogy Melville accomplished, in fact, the same end as the novelists who succeeded him. That is, he suggested as they did that personality is complex and that the mazes of behavior do not form a single and complete pattern. His anticipation of the next century's view of the individual is best expressed in *The Confidence-Man,* where he defended inconsistency as a mark of verisimilitude in the portrayal of character. But this conviction—that every man is an infinitely complicated phenomenon—is implicit in all his citations to secular and to Biblical individuals. His method in characterization was always suggestive rather than definitive.

And so, however distinctly they may stand in the relation of prototypes to Melville's characters, none of the Biblical figures he mentioned is in any sense the basis for an allegory. Of all the analogies suggested by them none is completely conceived or perfectly carried out; only a hint is given, a tradition implied. Upon complete application the pattern breaks down. The prophet Elijah is properly a part of the history of King Ahab, but in *Moby-Dick* the captain of the *Pequod* and the stammering soothsayer never meet. Pierre is a combination of two unrelated Biblical characters, but he represents neither completely. Though he is an incarnation of the gentle Jesus, Billy Budd strikes a man down to his death.

Nor are the lives of Melville's characters in any significant way influenced by the lives of their Biblical prototypes. Personalities are carried over, but not always corresponding events. So little interest did he have in reconstructing a second Ishmael in the sailor of the *Pequod* that Melville allowed the character virtually to disappear the moment Ahab entered the scene. And as for Ahab, he is destroyed through his own imprudent action, not because his character resembles in some remarkable particulars that of King Ahab. For a moment he is a counterpart of the Israelite monarch, but in that moment his fate is merely exalted, not explained.

In fact, Peleg's boast about Ahab may be applied to the whole host of Melville's characters. Affected as they are by Scriptural patterns, by literary and historical types, constituting, indeed, types themselves, each nonetheless achieves a life of his own. The impressionable Ishmael, about to sail the boundless seas under a strange captain, hears one of his proprietors say of him: " 'Oh! he ain't Captain Bildad; no, and he ain't Captain Peleg; *he's Ahab,* boy. . . .' "[55] So many parallels are necessary to describe Ahab because he matches none completely but is a spirit moving free and uncapturable through the world.

[55] *Moby-Dick,* I, 99.

Themes and Plots

THE OVERWEENING aspiration of all Melville's great characters is the measure of the great thematic purpose of their lives. For whether they seek the ideal form like Taji or the ideal action like Pierre, all are engaged in one intense, superhuman, eternal quest: the quest for the absolute amidst its relative manifestations. All Melville's plots describe this pursuit, and all his themes represent the delicate and shifting relationship between its truth and its illusion.

The metaphysical and even the moral implications of this quest are never entirely clear, for the reason that the two realms of thought were never distinct in Melville's mind. So thoroughly was his thought, like that of Emerson and Hawthorne, imbued with ethical precepts that he could not consider the world without them. Yet though he was reared in the same tradition of Platonism tempered by Protestant theology, he was incapable of coming to terms with it as they did. The forms of Calvinism did not content him, nor the formlessness of Transcendentalism. Had his philosophic background been Aristotelian or even Thomist, his natural bent toward a philosophical and a religious dualism might have been better satisfied; he might not have traveled so far and so wistfully to Palestine in 1856.

As it was, finding reality in both form and idea, in both good and evil, Melville's quest for the absolute led him to press beyond the realm in which these conceptions are mutually exclusive toward one in which they are halves of one whole. The Romantic tradition itself tried to do no less, and many of the themes Melville employed are borrowed from this source: the themes of unfulfilled love, of incest, of exile, of the hunt, of the ascent, of the duel.

Others he borrowed from the Bible. It is possible, of course, to consider as thematic certain images, characters, and stylistic devices which Melville derived thence, so frequent and so purposeful is their recurrence: the desert setting of Sinai or Paran, the expulsion from Eden, the Ishmael type, the Hebraic parallel and proverb. Aside from these fragments of design, however, four major Scriptural themes may be distinguished in his novels: the theme of prophecy in *Moby-Dick;* the theme of wisdom literature cursorily from *Mardi* to *Billy Budd;* the theme of the Gospel ethics in *Mardi, Pierre,* and *The Confidence-Man;* and the theme of the Crucifixion in *Billy Budd*.

I

The great motif that appears in *Moby-Dick* is prophecy. Innumerable prophetic patterns ornament the tale—the tablets in the Whalemen's Chapel, the name of Peter Coffin, Ahab's loss of his comforting pipe, the dropping of the trumpet from the hands of the *Albatross's* captain as he prepared to answer Ahab's query about Moby-Dick, the fish swimming away from Ahab and toward the *Albatross,* the *Pequod's* encounter with the mysterious squid, the fates of the *Jeroboam,* the *Samuel Enderby,* the *Rachel,* and the *Delight,* Fedallah's standing in Ahab's shadow, Ahab's construction of another log and line, and his regulation of the thunderstruck compass. But in addition to these omens and implications there are articulate prophets in the book:

the squaw Tistig, Father Mapple, Elijah, Gabriel, and
Fedallah. And the entire story may be said to be the account of the fulfilment of their prophecies.

Now these prophets belong to a particular school of
prophecy: the Hebrew. All but Fedallah are verbally connected with some Old Testament prophet or prophecy, and
Father Mapple has even caught the idiom of that speech.
In fact, Melville seems to have associated the whole prophetic profession with the Hebrews. With his penchant for
the particular rather than the general, he referred to " 'the
Hebrew prophets' " and a "prophet of Israel"[1] when his
context called for only the common noun.

He seems to have distinguished, too, among these prophets of Israel. For the prophets in *Moby-Dick*, who are by
no means of equal stature—some are eloquent, some are
mere sound and fury—correspond to certain definite types
among the Hebrews. It is the emergence of these types,
in fact, which constitutes the chief development of their
prophecy. Usually said to have three stages, it begins with
the simple soothsayer, or foreteller, like the Witch of Endor.
Such prophets are the Gay Head Indian Tistig and Elijah.
Both, in general but unmistakable terms, foretell Ahab's
death; and Elijah includes in his fate all who are associated
with him. This kind of prophecy may be followed out
by succeeding events in history, which, in *Moby-Dick*, thoroughly vindicate these crude seers.

As it became more sophisticated, Hebrew prophecy
reached its culmination in the person of the interpreter or
spokesman of Jehovah, such as Amos, Hosea, and Isaiah.
Father Mapple is this type of prophet. In his sermon to the
whalemen he endeavors as no other person in all Melville's
novels to illuminate and rationalize the workings of an apparently blind fate. Even the text of his discourse is in
keeping with his character: the story of the prophet Jonah.

[1] *Billy Budd and Other Prose Pieces*, p. 45; *Poems*, p. 188.

Declining at last into an apocalyptic type of foretelling, Hebrew prophecy in its later phase is best represented by the last part of the Book of Daniel. Unlike the soothsayer, the apocalyptic foreteller cannot be vindicated by history; he speaks of things which do not happen in time. To this class of prophets Gabriel belongs. He not only narrates events which may be verified, such as the death of Macey, but he claims knowledge of facts which are beyond proof: he insists upon his own archangelic identity and recognizes in Moby-Dick the incarnation of his Shaker God.

Besides individuals such as these, who are all true prophets, there appeared among the Hebrews equivocal or false prophets. The subject is an obscure one, complicated by the fact that such prophets might be deliberately misled by Jehovah, as were those of Ahab's court. Even the fulfilment of the prophecy was not always adduced as a test, though it remained the popular one. Actually, the main distinction between the true and false prophets seems to have been a moral or spiritual one, founded upon the individual's intent, and thus not immediately perceptible. So Fedallah may be said to belong to this class of prophets. For although his predictions to Ahab are verified by events in the last chapter of *Moby-Dick,* he plays a false role with his captain, luring him to his death with apparent promises of success.

The oracular nature of Fedallah's speech, it is true, is somewhat reminiscent of Greek prophecy, a school to which Melville occasionally referred figuratively but which he came no nearer imitating than this. Had he been less saturated with the tradition of the Bible he might have associated the insanity which he occasionally bestowed on his prophets with Greek rather than Hebrew thought. Unlike Jehovah's spokesmen, the oracles of the Olympian gods were often as enigmatical to themselves as to their hearers. But between the mad priestesses of Delphi and Dodona and

Melville's cracked Elijah and Gabriel there is no connection.
His conception of the unseen world was not Greek. If the
gods choose to speak, Starbuck observes, "'they will hon-
ourably speak outright; not shake their heads, and give an
old wives' darkling hint.'"[2]

It is largely the presence of these prophetic characters
which creates in *Moby-Dick* its mood of fate—a mood pervading so many of Melville's books. For like the Hebrew
prophets, hopelessly entangled in their national destiny,
these individuals are defeatists, first to last, prophesying ill
fortune for a mischosen course. It is not so with another
school of prophecy which Melville also knew: the eight-
eenth-century American Indian prophets. To Indian culture in general—its wars, tribes, wigwams, sachems, and
famous individuals—he frequently referred. It was one
aspect of the primitivism in which he had an abiding interest. But its prophets, chief among them the Delaware,
Munsee, and Shawnee prophets, were far too optimistic
for him; part of their message was the confident notion
that the Redman would reconquer the continent.

One of the great Hebrew messages of doom, on the
other hand, reverberates throughout *Moby-Dick*. It is the
prophecy that the commercial states of Phoenicia, Tyre and
Sidon, would be destroyed[3]—a prediction the more remarkable because history had not thus far pointed to the pre-
carious nature of a mercantile economy or to its possible
downfall. Melville later marked Stanley's discussion of
this subject in his copy of *Sinai and Palestine,* and in his
own Bible he underscored the word "merchants" in Job
41:6: ". . . shall they part him [leviathan] among the
merchants?"

The story of King Ahab itself is illustrative of this
theme, since the prophets of his court opposed his trade

[2] *Moby-Dick,* II, 341.
[3] Isa. 23:1, 15; Ezek. 26-28.

with the heathen Ben-hadad. It is a detail of the narrative
which in *Moby-Dick* undergoes a characteristic metamor-
phosis. Actually the catastrophe overwhelming the *Pequod*
is the result not of the commercial purpose of her voyage
but of that purpose's being abandoned. Yet so quickly and
so far behind are the claims of trade left that they are in
effect totally irrelevant. The whaling enterprise is of no
more genuine consequence than King Ahab's bazaars or
Phoenicia's ships, while Captain Ahab's "fiery hunt" goes
eternally on, in a realm in which Father Mapple and the
Old Testament seers are equally at home.

For if most of Melville's pessimistic prophets in *Moby-
Dick* dwell exclusively upon the horror of the forthcoming
catastrophe, ignoring its significance and its original cause,
one does not. Father Mapple has a conception of the law
itself which underlies the whole narrative. He thus embodies the true purpose of Hebrew prophecy, which is
revelation, not mystery-mongering. From his seaworthy
pulpit in the Whalemen's Chapel he not only issues a warning of destruction, but he defines the fundamental statute
which, once broken, precipitates that destruction.

For his text on this occasion the resourceful Mapple
turns to the one book in the Bible written for an audience
of whalemen. The choice is nothing less than inspired.
But the appropriateness of its selection and the arresting
nautical idiom in which it is retold cannot hide the fact
that between this tale and the theme of Father Mapple's
discourse there is the greatest discrepancy. Far from illustrating his philosophy, it is the best example in all the Old
Testament to support the opposite point of view.

As Mapple pictures him, Jonah himself is a kind of Ishmael, called to set himself against the city of Nineveh by
warning the populace that for their sins they are about to
be destroyed. Being unwilling to obey, he takes ship to escape from Jehovah. Thus far Mapple follows the Biblical

story. But in assigning a motive for Jonah's flight he diverges from it. In the last chapter of the Book of Jonah the prophet makes a clear defense of himself when he professes to have known that Jehovah's heart was soft and to have suspected that the divine decree for their destruction would be revoked if the wicked Ninevites were moved by his preaching to repentance. Therefore, in order to avoid seeing his prophecy so controverted, he embarked for Tarshish. His suspicions have been vindicated; he has threatened Nineveh with destruction, the people have repented, and Jehovah, touched by their renewed allegiance to him, has pardoned them. The prophet appears to himself vain and even ridiculous. But more than that, he can but appear sadly primitive by the side of this compassionate Jehovah, the immediate forerunner of the New Testament Father.

It is an entirely different motive which is ascribed to Jonah's flight by Father Mapple. His Jonah has none of the vindictive spirit of the fire-eating Biblical prophet; on the contrary, he shrinks from preaching a doctrine of destruction because of the enemies he will create. Realizing how unwelcome the truth of the Lord will be to the wicked city, he is appalled to think of the hostility he will raise there. And for this reason he flees from the very land, hoping to escape his duty. But even in his flight he becomes the thing he wishes to escape becoming: an outcast among his fellows, bringing hatred upon himself in their midst. Even nature conspires against him, brewing up such a gale that the crew is forced to sacrifice him for its own safety. His only recourse now being to accept the will of Jehovah, Jonah repents of his disobedience and sets out for Nineveh.

Like Josephus, Father Mapple omits the last of Jonah's story. There is nothing in his sermon about Jehovah's compassion for the repentant city, his pardon, and his gentle remonstrance with his harsh prophet. This final chapter of the book, as the most casual reader will agree, is its heart and its beauty. To it Melville cannot have been insensitive or, like the Pharisaic Josephus, opposed. But the structure of *Moby-Dick* calls for the sermon and the narrative to agree, and in the tragic voyage of the *Pequod* there is no divine interference.

Father Mapple's story of Jonah, then, is not the one related by the Biblical scribe. But it is substantially the story of another Old Testament prophet: Jeremiah. Among the four great prophets his name appears least often in Melville's pages—less than half a dozen times in all. Yet in itself this fact may signify little. Melville was often at pains to disguise and even to disavow his sources, as he claimed, for example, never to have seen a copy of Porter's *Cruise,* upon which he drew for *Typee.* That he read Jeremiah is attested by the well-marked pages of this book in his Bible, where he also marked the prophecies of Isaiah, Ezekiel, Daniel, Joel, Jonah, and Habakkuk. The details of Jeremiah's life, however, would seem to have had a peculiar appeal for him.

It is, in some respects, the noblest life in the Old Testament. The divine call to prophecy found Jeremiah a diffident and reluctant young man, unlike Ezekiel, for instance, shrinking from Jehovah's harsh role for him, which was to be "a defenced city, and an iron pillar, and brasen walls against the whole land, against the kings of Judah, against the princes thereof, against the priests thereof, and against the people of the land."[4] For something like twenty years his sensitive nature, even while obeying, struggled against this divine plan, and his contest with kings and princes was accompanied by an interior battle. Such, in fact, is the character ascribed by Father Mapple to the quite dissimiliar prophet Jonah.

Indeed, the times in which Jeremiah lived are more aptly described as divinely "brewed . . . into a gale, as

[4] Jer. 1:18.

Mapple puts it, than Jonah's eighth century. It was, in the southern kingdom, the time of the first Babylonian captivity. Forced into silence during a temporary period of national prosperity, Jeremiah emerged to prophesy that Jehovah would destroy the Temple at Jerusalem. For this inflammatory speech he nearly lost his life, being first put in the stocks by the priests and later imprisoned by the princes.

His soliloquy on the first occasion marked the climax of his long mental conflict, and in it he acknowledged the bitter truth which is also Father Mapple's discovery: that peace with the world is unattainable by the man with a divinely appointed task. When he follows Jehovah's command he is maltreated, yet forsake it he cannot. He has tried. And he is constrained not by any external action of Jehovah's, as in the case of Jonah, but by some inner necessity—like that of Ahab:

O Lord, thou hast deceived me, and I was deceived: thou art stronger than I, and hast prevailed: I am in derision daily, every one mocketh me.

For since I spake, I cried out, I cried violence and spoil; because the word of the Lord was made a reproach unto me, and a derision daily.

Then I said, I will not make mention of him, nor speak any more in his name. But his word was in mine heart as a burning fire shut up in my bones, and I was weary with forbearing and I could not stay.[5]

Not the least element in Jeremiah's painful renunciation of the world is Jehovah's demand, not made on Hosea, for example, for his celibacy. His imagination is haunted, like Ahab's, by the thought of his home, and often the image of the bridegroom's voice stilled by Jehovah appears on his pages. Melville marked one of the passages in his own Bible: "Then will I cause to cease from the cities of Judah,

[5] Jer. 20:7-9.

and from the streets of Jerusalem, the voice of mirth, and
the voice of gladness, the voice of the bridegroom, and the
voice of the bride: for the land shall be desolate."[6]

Nor is Ahab the only one of Melville's heroes called
upon to abandon domestic happiness. More than the senti-
mental unfulfilment of romantic love, this is a deliberate
sacrifice, a necessary part of the great renunciation of all
penultimate truths, if the ultimate is indeed to be found.
Each man must proceed alone. So from Taji's bower in
Odo the elusive Yillah disappears, and Pierre abandons his
fiancée Lucy for his half-sister Isabel. Clarel makes his
pilgrimage without Ruth and hears the celibate at Mar Saba
enjoin him:

> In the pure desert of the will
> Chastised, live the vowed life austere,[7]

citing meanwhile the examples of

> . . . David's son [Amnon], and he of Dan [Samson],
> With him misloved that fled the bride [Joseph],
> And Job whose wife but mocked his ban;
> Then rose, or in redemption ran—
> The rib restored to Adam's side,
> And man made whole, as man began.[8]

Even the family of the unwilling Starbuck is bereft in the
final wreck of the *Pequod,* whose captain had observed:
". . . even the highest earthly felicities ever have a certain un-
signifying pettiness lurking in them. . . ."[9]

Unmistakably Jeremiah was no ordinary prophet of
gloom, and his sermon regarding the fall of the Temple,
for which he was apprehended, was no ordinary prophecy
of disaster. It was his contention that Jehovah purposed to
destroy the structure not as a punishment but in the interest of true religion—at first glance a blasphemous and a

---

[6] *Ibid.,* 7:34.   [7] *Clarel,* II, 145.
[8] *Ibid.*   [9] *Moby-Dick,* II, 230.

traitorous idea. But the Deuteronomic reform of King Josiah, by making the Temple the one legitimate center of worship, had formalized and nationalized religion, and it was Jeremiah's purpose to disembody it. As the sanctuary at Shiloh had been destroyed, said he, so it was necessary for Jerusalem to be devastated before the true spiritual nature of religion could be realized. Transferring his theory to politics, Jeremiah assumed the role also of traitor by recognizing Babylon, against which Josiah's court constantly rebelled, as nothing less than a benevolent agent of Jehovah, by means of which his plan for Judah was to be accomplished.

This plan, it must be emphasized, was by no means narrowly retributive. In connection with Father Mapple's sermon, and with Melville's thought in general, it was most significantly a plan of salvation. Despite the melancholy associations which cluster round Jeremiah's name—Melville himself referred to "Jeremiads"—he had the valorous confidence which only a prophet of the spirit can have. Writing to the exiles in Babylon, he urged them to cease all efforts to return to Jerusalem, since by reducing them to dependence upon him there Jehovah purposed to reveal himself to them: "Thus saith the LORD, The people which were left of the sword found grace in the wilderness; even Israel, when I went to cause him to rest."[10] In fact, the salvation of Israel through captivity in Babylon was to follow an earlier pattern: Jehovah's revelation of himself to the tribes in the Exodus. This episode of his national history is the source of Jeremiah's figure of speech, for he quoted Jehovah as saying:

I remember thee, the kindness of thy youth, the love of thine espousals, when thou wentest after me in the wilderness, in a land that was not sown. . . .

Neither said they, Where is the LORD that brought us up out of the land of Egypt, that led us through the wilderness, through

[10] Jer. 31:2.

a land of deserts and of pits, through a land of drought, and
of the shadow of death, through a land that no man passed
through, and where no man dwelt?[11]

Both verses are marked in Melville's Bible.

The religion envisaged by Jeremiah thus promised on
the one hand freedom of the individual spirit and on the
other the gravest personal peril. Unfettered by ecclesiasti-
cal or political institutions, it was, in the widest sense of
the word, spiritual, as unbounded as Melville's sea, as bodi-
less as his air. The old law of "the sins of the fathers" is
superseded by a "new covenant" with each individual. It
is the beginning of the New Testament doctrine of personal
salvation, quoted by Jesus himself. The law is now written
in the heart of a man:

After those days, saith the LORD, I will put my law in their
inward parts, and write it in their hearts; and will be their God,
and they shall be my people.

And they shall teach no more every man his neighbour, and
every man his brother, saying, Know the LORD: for they shall
all know me, from the least of them unto the greatest of them,
saith the LORD. . . .[12]

The verses call to mind not only the self-determining Ahab
in *Moby-Dick,* but also Pierre and Billy Budd, whose inner
law Melville so passionately contrasted with that without.
Old Bardianna even echoes the words of Jeremiah when he
says: "'. . . we need not be told what righteousness is; we
were born with the whole Law in our hearts.'"[13]

At the same time, the tragic circumstances of his age
led Jeremiah more than any other Old Testament prophet
to associate also an element of peril with any plan of redemption. And so it is with Melville. The way of truth is

[11] *Ibid.,* 2:2, 6.
[12] *Ibid.,* 31:33, 34.
[13] *Mardi,* II, 303.

uneasy, lonely, and fraught with mortal danger. Even the whale, as Ishmael observes, is best comprehended in his own frightful element:

ı How vain and foolish, then, thought I, for timid untravelled man to try to comprehend aright this wondrous whale, by merely poring over his dead attenuated skeleton, stretched in this peaceful wood. No. Only in the heart of quickest perils; only when within the eddyings of his angry flukes; only on the profound unbounded sea, can the fully invested whale be truly and livingly found out.[14]

Without doubt an excursion into the life of Jeremiah illuminates the theme of Father Mapple's sermon as the story of Jonah does not. But neither can the *tour de force* of introducing *Moby-Dick* with the greatest of all whale yarns be improved upon. The loss in literary accuracy is a spectacular artistic gain, and it is with singular dexterity that the lives of the two prophets are entwined.

As Father Mapple tells them, Jonah's adventures illustrate the operation of a destiny which, once set in motion, the individual cannot control or escape. The determination of Jehovah to send Jonah to Nineveh was not to be disputed; even the physical universe plotted to bring about the accomplishment of that purpose. And since Father Mapple is himself a prophet of sorts, the same inexorable fate may be seen operating in the lives of the characters who people *Moby-Dick*—and, for that matter, of all Melville's characters.

But, unlike Jonah, none of them is interfered with by an external force. There is nothing in all Melville's narratives comparable in function to the whale. His notion of tragedy as interior is in the Renaissance rather than the classical tradition, for the force which moves all his major characters is their own. They are like Jeremiah, impelled

[14] *Moby-Dick*, II, 218.

from within, resolving for his own health not to speak Jehovah's word, yet finding it impossible to be silent. Its fire consumed his bones, as the Persian fire of Ahab's desire burned in him.

Again, returning to Jonah, Melville found there an element of his theme which is not in Jeremiah. It is the notion that this inexorable fate is amoral. It is neither controlled by wisdom nor tempered to innocence. The crew of Jonah's vessel would have been destroyed with him had they not separated their lots from his. So the crew of the *Pequod,* ignoring the example, perish with their captain. For though Starbuck perceives the whole terrible scheme of affairs, how in Ahab's precipitate flight to destruction the entire crew is drawn along, he is powerless to alter the situation. Like Pierre, with whom both Lucy and Isabel are sacrificed and whose catastrophe is described in the same figure of speech, he sees that "in tremendous extremities human souls are like drowning men; well enough they know they are in peril; well enough they know the causes of that peril; nevertheless, the sea is the sea, and these drowning men do drown."[15]

Nor is this destiny, as both Jonah and Jeremiah knew, in any way colored by the emotions of men. It is neither tragic nor happy. It does not matter that Jonah was called to be a prophet with an unwelcome message; that Jeremiah was called to bring upon himself derision, calumny, hatred, imprisonment. It does not matter that some persons are called to be Ishmaels against the world. Indeed, there is no happiness except in submission to this will and no misfortune except in the attempt to escape it. As Father Mapple cries:

"Woe to him whom this world charms from Gospel duty! Woe to him who seeks to pour oil upon the waters when God has brewed them into a gale! Woe to him who seeks to please rather than to appal! Woe to him whose good name is more to him than goodness! Woe to him who, in this world, courts

<hr />

[15] *Pierre,* p. 423.

not dishonour! Woe to him who would not be true, even though to be false were salvation! Yea, woe to him who, as the great Pilot Paul has it, while preaching to others is himself a castaway!"[16]

In this overpowering denunciation Mapple turns for example to the storm which overtook Jonah. He could have found an equally awesome one in Jeremiah's prophecy of the seventy years of captivity, a passage Melville penciled in his Bible.

But now the sermon in the Whalemen's Chapel passes from negation and concludes on a note of wild exultation. And now, finally, it is Jeremiah, with his prophecy that the captives will at length return, who provides the parallel; Melville marked the famous consolation of Chapter 30 as he read it. If one fully acquiesces in this will of the universe, then all the apparent misfortunes of life become transformed into the most exquisite delights. They are, as the man in Stubb's dream remarks, kicks with an ivory leg instead of a common pitch-pine one, and so to be considered honorable.

This is no ordinary happiness. But for characters such as Ahab, Pierre, Taji, Budd, even Media and Nathan common joy does not exist. In its place is a higher, more poignant sense of satisfaction in fulfilling their separate destinies. Each of them could be described by the words which Melville copied on a fly leaf of his New Testament:

In Life he appears as a true Philosopher—as a wise man in the highest sense. He stands firm to his point; he goes on his way inflexibly; and while he exalts the lower to himself, while he makes the ignorant, the poor, the sick, partakers of his wisdom, of his riches, of his strength, he, on the other hand, in no wise conceals his divine origin; he dares to equal himself with God; nay, to declare that he himself is God.

[16] *Moby-Dick*, I, 58-59.

Each testifies to the truth of Father Mapple's eloquent conclusion:

"Delight is to him—a far, far, upward, and inward delight—who against the proud gods and commodores of this earth, ever stands forth his own inexorable self. Delight is to him whose strong arms yet support him, when the ship of this base treacherous world has gone down beneath him. Delight is to him, who gives no quarter in the truth, and kills, burns, and destroys all sin though he pluck it out from under the robes of Senators and Judges. Delight,—top-gallant delight is to him, who acknowledges no law or lord, but the Lord his God, and is only a patriot to heaven. Delight is to him, whom all the waves of the billows of the seas of the boisterous mob can never shake from this sure Keel of the Ages. And eternal delight and deliciousness will be his, who coming to lay him down, can say with his final breath—O Father!—chiefly known to me by Thy rod—mortal or immortal, here I die. I have striven to be Thine, more than to be this world's, or mine own. Yet this is nothing; I leave eternity to Thee; for what is man that he should live out the lifetime of his God?"[17]

Father Mapple's sermon, then, not merely contributes to the prophetic atmosphere at the beginning of *Moby-Dick*, but it constitutes in itself a prophecy, of which the ensuing narrative is a fulfilment. If there is any doubt about the matter, the last vessel seen by the *Pequod* dispels it. She is the *Delight*, her stove boats and splintered sides mocking her name and publishing to all whalers what an encounter with the white whale means. Surely the name she bears is significant. It is an echo from the conclusion of Father Mapple's sermon in distant New Bedford. The same word ends the prophecy and ends its fulfilment. And far more dramatically than even he could have told, this sorry ship represents the paradox of that word as he used it. For the delight which the uncompromising follower of

[17] *Ibid.*, I, 59.

the truth will have is a delight not of this world, but invisible, in the heart.

Yet the *Delight* is not the last ship of all in *Moby-Dick;* there is, finally, the *Rachel.* And her name, if not an echo of Mapple's sermon, is an echo from Jeremiah. For the verse which is paraphrased in the concluding sentence of the book comes from the prophet's great oracle of consolation, the promise that the exiles will return:

> Thus saith the LORD; A voice was heard in Ramah, lamentation, and bitter weeping; Rachel weeping for her children refused to be comforted for her children, because they were not.
> Thus saith the Lord; Refrain thy voice from weeping, and thine eyes from tears: for thy work shall be rewarded, saith the LORD; and they shall come again from the land of the enemy.[18]

This is the ship which, rescuing the sailor Ishmael, keeps the fate of the *Pequod* from being quite the final word.

This spiritual consolation, this interior delight is the reward of all Melville's prophets and heroes. Yet all the while they advance boldly into the wasteland, they look back with tenderness and longing to the green, companionable glades. So the Israelites in the Exodus looked to Egypt. The hymn which rightfully accompanies Father Mapple's sermon is separated from it by several chapters and belongs to a different occasion, but its mixed mood is the same. Bildad leads, as the *Pequod* casts off into the deep:

> "Sweet fields beyond the swelling flood,
>   Stand dressed in living green.
> So to the Jews old Canaan stood,
>   While Jordan rolled between."[19]

II

The prophets of the Old Testament were undeviating in their single purpose, but not so the authors of the wisdom

[18] Jer. 31:15-16.
[19] *Moby-Dick,* I, 129.

books. And side by side with the theme of prophecy in Melville's pages is the theme of their equivocal thought. Ahab and Pierre, Taji and Billy Budd will not compromise, but it is the nature of such characters as Babbalanja, Bildad, Starbuck, Falsgrave, Plinlimmon to vary with the moral times. It is significant that all these characters are minor. Yet none of Melville's major characters is without one or more of them as foils. For the absolute which his heroes seek can be pictured only by contrast; there is no comparison.

Being thus so often juxtaposed with other themes, the thought of the wisdom writers is more cursory in Melville's narratives than any other thought of the Old Testament. No other group of Scriptural books is so extensively represented in his pages, or so profusely marked in his Bible. True, these books comprise a small group. But with the exception of the Wisdom of Solomon, Melville alludes to and quotes from them all: Job, Proverbs, Ecclesiastes, Ecclesiasticus. At the same time he marked passages in each, and noted wisdom sentiments also in Psalms and II Esdras.

These five books constitute the great legacy of the sages, who supplanted the prophets in postexilic Israel, and whose general disposition to temporize arises perhaps from the fact that their difficult problem was to reconcile Judaism with Western culture. Their position in history, however, and the fine distinctions between them as individuals Melville ignored; he differentiated much more between the prophets in his casual allusions to Isaiah, Daniel, Jeremiah. Like the rest of his generation, he attributed two of the wisdom books, together with the Song of Solomon, to the traditional author, Solomon.

But he also generalized about their content, where he might have made many distinctions for himself, distinctions such as he noted Schopenhauer making in *The Wisdom of Life* between Ecclesiastes and Ecclesiasticus. The superficial optimism of Proverbs, the skepticism of Ecclesiastes, the deeper questionings of Job, the ethical mean of Ecclesiasticus—all appear side by side in his allusions as expressions of one pre-eminently secular and deeply shadowed philosophy. The absence of the Wisdom of Solomon, with its elements of Greek mysticism, is significant. "Solomonic" is his synonym for the word *disillusioned,* and the sentiments he freely ascribed to the monarch are of the most general pessimistic nature. A characterization of him by Ishmael is typical of many, perhaps prompted by such words as these of the Preacher, which he marked in his Bible: "The heart of the wise is in the house of mourning; but the heart of fools is in the house of mirth."[20] Wrote Ishmael:

The truest of all men was the Man of Sorrows, and the truest of all books is Solomon's, and Ecclesiastes is the fine hammered steel of woe. "All is vanity." ALL. This wilful world hath not got hold of unchristian Solomon's wisdom yet. But he who dodges hospitals and jails, and walks fast crossing graveyards, and would rather talk of operas than hell; calls Cooper, Young, Pascal, Rousseau, poor devils all of sick men; and throughout a care-free lifetime swears by Rabelais as passing wise, and therefore jolly;—not that man is fitted to sit down on tombstones, and break the green damp mould with unfathomably wondrous Solomon.

But even Solomon, he says, "the man that wandereth out of the way of understanding shall remain" (*i.e.* even while living) "in the congregation of the dead."[21]

It scarcely needs to be observed that nearly all Melville's characters, at one time or another, have fits of depression in which they share the pessimism of the Old Testament skeptics. But when he spoke of it as a system of thought rather than a passing mood, Melville, unlike

[20] Eccles. 7:4.
[21] *Moby-Dick,* II, 181-182. The quoted verse is marked in Melville's Bible.

Elihu, whose definition of wisdom as "a spirit in man" he marked, inclined to call this wisdom the product of maturity rather than of individuality. Apparently he thought of the material in the Gospels as being especially tempered to adolescence, whereas the Old Testament held more significance for age. At the beginning of *Pierre*, the hero is still at that period in his development when "the Solomonic insights have not poured their turbid tributaries into the pure-flowing well of the childish life."[22] On the other hand, Pierre's old kinsman, "after a long and richly varied, but unfortunate life, had at last found great solace in the Old Testament, which he was continually studying with ever-increasing admiration. . . ."[23]

This oldster may in fact be repeating Melville's own experience. In 1851 he wrote to Hawthorne:

I have come to regard this matter of Fame as the most transparent of all vanities. I read Solomon more and more, and every time see deeper and deeper and unspeakable meanings in him. I did not think of Fame, a year ago, as I do now. . . . It seems to me now that Solomon was the truest man that ever spoke, and yet that he a little *managed* the truth with a view to popular conservatism; or else there have been many corruptions and interpolations of the text.[24]

And in the novels of his maturity, especially those written after *Moby-Dick*, the wisdom theme occurs more often.

If he did not distinguish between their individual moods, Melville did recognize in the wisdom books the two separate lines of thought which characterize the whole school: it had both a human and a divine argument. It is not, however, as this duality suggests, a philosophy in the true sense of the word, a fact which may explain the extent to which it pervades Melville's books. No strict system of thought seems ever to have taken hold of him.

[22] *Pierre*, pp. 93-94.   [23] *Ibid.*, p. 187.
[24] [June 1851] (*Representative Selections*, pp. 392-393).

The human aspect of wisdom, as the Hebrews thought of it, was strictly utilitarian. Admitting no revelation, it grounded its maxims in universal principles of human nature and the conditions necessary for a successful life. The adaptation of this practicality to the heritage of righteousness received from the prophets inevitably produced an equivocal moral code. The general thesis, as propounded in Proverbs, was that prosperity is the reward of piety, but since success was the end, virtue was only one of many means. Since, as the Preacher perceived, the moral seasons change, a man must change with them. Mediocrity is his most prudent course, and consequently even his friends must be continually suspicious of his action.

Without doubt the most familiar aspect to Melville of this human wisdom of the Hebrews was its economic theory: the godly prosper. It was part of the Puritanism of his heritage, continuing throughout the nineteenth century to be one of the most heavily emphasized themes in all Scripture. Its greatest American proponent Melville sketched in *Israel Potter,* where, in fact, Benjamin Franklin has the role of shrewd sage elsewhere in Melville's novels given a definite association with Old Testament Scripture.

That Melville knew this theory's source in the Bible, moreover, is attested by the name he gave Captain Bildad, and by his comparison of Old Prudence and Old Plain Talk in China Aster's story to Job's three friends. And that he held it to be a fallacious theory is only too apparent in the fates of all his heroes, who, though obeying their best impulses, perish miserably. Throughout the Old Testament books of his Bible he noted the paradoxical observations, especially in Job, Psalms, and Ecclesiastes, on the one hand that the ungodly are like the chaff and on the other that the race is not to the swift.

Next to this economic thesis of the Hebrew sages Melville seems to have been most impressed by their theory of times and seasons. He noted the great exposition of it in the third chapter of Ecclesiastes and also the passage in the fourth chapter of II Esdras, where the archangel Uriel describes evil in terms of a harvest springing from a seed. Even its origins in the thought of the prophets caught his attention, influencing him in *Moby-Dick* to echo the prophetic version of Jehovah's dispensations: an oracle of doom followed by one of consolation.

But other theses of the Hebrew sages Melville knew as well as these, and almost no novel is without its advocate of them. In *Mardi* there are two such advocates: Babbalanja and his constant authority, the sage Bardianna. Bardianna's *Ponderings,* if not in the style of Solomon, contains discourses on many Solomonic subjects: the superficiality of fame, the finality of death, the authority of reason, which " 'was the first revelation; and so far as it tests all others, it has precedence over them.' "[25] All who read Bardianna, boasts his disciple, " 'feast at the tables of Wisdom.' "[26]

Without question Babbalanja himself has read Solomon, for he readily falls into the idiom of Ecclesiastes. " 'All vanity, vanity, Yoomy,' "[27] he declares when the poet seeks a proof in nature of human immortality. He paraphrases the same author's verses on the repetitious nature of events. Exclaimed the Preacher, in a passage marked by Melville:

The sun also ariseth, and the sun goeth down, and hasteth to his place where he arose. . . .

All things are full of labour; man cannot utter it: the eye is not satisfied with seeing, nor the ear filled with hearing.

The thing that hath been, it is that which shall be; and that which is done is that which shall be done: and there is no new thing under the sun.

Is there any thing whereof it may be said, See, this is new? it hath been already of old time, which was before us.[28]

[25] *Mardi,* II, 301.
[27] *Ibid.,* I, 244.
[26] *Ibid.,* II, 305.
[28] Eccles. 1:5, 8-10.

Babbalanja says to Media:

"Tell us, ye sages! something worth an archangel's learning; discover, ye discoverers, something new. Fools, fools! Mardi's not changed: the sun yet rises in its old place in the East; all things go on in the same old way. . . . Nothing changes, though much be new-fashioned: new fashions but revivals of things previous. In the books of the past we learn naught but of the present; in those of the present, the past."[29]

In defining infinity in terms of human follies Babbalanja is as cynical as the twenty-sixth chapter of Proverbs on fools, and he is as wily in his rules of etiquette as the preceding chapter of the same book. A true skeptic, he has a variety of marvelous tales to illustrate the relativity of truth and the transforming power of time. His definition of religion is strictly in terms of this world:

"My lord! my lord! out of itself, Religion has nothing to bestow. Nor will she save us from aught, but from the evil in ourselves. Her one grand end is to make us wise; her only manifestations are reverence to Oro and love to man; her only, but ample reward, herself."[30]

It is a definition which is akin to if not actually derived from the Hebrew sages: "Let us hear the conclusion of the whole matter: Fear God, and keep his commandments: for this is the whole duty of man."[31]

In *Pierre* the chief exponent of the wisdom school is Plotinus Plinlimmon, whose metaphor of "Chronometricals and Horologicals" recalls the Preacher's theory of time. Aside from this fact, the "virtuous expediency" which he advocates is explained in terms of the New rather than the Old Testament, since the central thesis of the book is phrased in these terms. But the equivocal code of Plinlimmon and Falsgrave, with which Pierre is confronted, has

[29] *Mardi*, II, 306, 307.
[30] *Ibid.*, II, 79-80.
[31] Eccles. 12:13. See also Job 28:28 and Prov. 1:7, which Melville marked.

everything in common with wisdom ethics. Falsgrave characterizes Mrs. Glendinning as an overheated champion of virtue and Pierre as too cold, as though he might be remembering words which Melville marked in his Bible:

> Be not righteous over much; neither make thyself over wise: why shouldest thou destroy thyself?
>
> Be not over much wicked, neither be thou foolish: why shouldest thou die before thy time?[32]

His brooch depicts the best New Testament allegory of this Old Testament sentiment: a carved union of the serpent and the dove.

With the episode of the Memnon stone, however, the philosophical opposition to Pierre is unmistakably associated with Old Testament wisdom. This antique structure Pierre fancies he is first to discover, until he sees the initials "S. ye W." upon it. His elderly kinsman, an Old Testament scholar, identifies them as standing for "Solomon the Wise" —but not without first "reading certain verses in Ecclesiastes." Amused at this notion, Pierre calls the rock instead the Memnon or the Terror stone. Lying beneath its precariously balanced end, he challenges it to fall upon him if his burning idealism is indeed destined to destroy him. His words, appropriately enough, are a paraphrase of the philosophy of "Solomon":

". . . if to vow myself all Virtue's and all Truth's, be but to make a trembling, distrusted slave of me; . . . if Life be a cheating dream, and virtue as unmeaning and unsequelled with any blessing as the midnight mirth of wine; . . . if Duty's self be but a bugbear, and all things are allowable and unpunishable to man;—then do thou, Mute Massiveness, fall on me!"[33]

The rock does not fall. But when Pierre afterwards remembers it, and his youthful whim to secure a piece of it

[32] Eccles. 7:16-17. In his Bible Melville substituted "be desolate" for the words "destroy thyself."

[33] *Pierre*, p. 189.

for his gravestone, the incident seems to him prophetic. For in the words which he addressed to the stone he unwittingly pronounced the formula for his own salvation. Had he then proceeded, with the Preacher, on the assumption that "virtue . . . [is] unsequelled with any blessing," his end might have been different. As he carried Plinlimmon's pamphlet in the lining of his coat without knowing it, so he lay beneath the stone of Solomon and repeated his worldly wisdom all unaware of its power to save him. His desire to have his grave marked by a fragment of the rock is, incidentally, a touch not unlike that of China Aster's epitaph, with its reference to "THE SOBER PHILOSOPHY OF SOLOMON THE WISE." The careers of both seem to bear witness that the man who attempts to live in this world without modifying his behavior by expediency is destined for an early death.

Most bitter of all sentiments of the wisdom writers with regard to humanity is their distrust of men. Melville noted dozens of verses, in Job, Psalms, and Ecclesiastes especially, referring to the deceit, the flattery, and the poor comfort of friends, and made passing allusions in most of his narratives to the rarity of true understanding. In *The Confidence-Man,* however, this is the central theme, amply illustrated by Scriptural allusions. In the latter part of the book particularly the characters converse by quoting from Ecclesiasticus, an antiphonal conclusion to the volume, which opens with excerpts from the thirteenth chapter of I Corinthians.

In this book, however, the wisdom theme receives the ironic treatment of being first presented in the guise of New Testament good will. The discrepancy between Christian theory and practice, more critically considered elsewhere by Melville, is here, like the discrepancy between any ideal philosophy and the testimony of experience, the chief *raison d'être* of a distinctly worldly wisdom. So each of the Confidence-Man's eight avatars is delineated with some reference to the New Testament, while the character of each belies these same words.

Introducing them is the deaf-mute, who reminds his fellow-travelers of Jacob sleeping at Luz, a meek, "lamb-like" creature, in perfect harmony with Melville's other pictures of theoretical Christianity, who writes on his slate several verses from the thirteenth chapter of I Corinthians. The next three manifestations of the Confidence-Man represent three character types from the Beatitudes: the Negro Black Guinea, who solicits alms, the poor in spirit; John Ringman, the man with the weed, those who mourn; the man with the gray coat, those who hunger and thirst after righteousness. The description of this last individual in particular abounds in Biblical allusions: he has a "not un-silvery tongue," a "Pentecost" of gestures, " 'confidence to remove obstacles, though mountains' ";[34] and for the woman who donates $20 to his cause he quotes Paul, " ' "I have confidence in you in all things." ' "[35] The man with the gold sleeve buttons whom he meets is contrasted with him by other words of the Apostle, " '. . . "scarcely for a righteous man will one die, yet peradventure for a good man some would even dare to die". . . .' " Because he relies on his black servant for menial tasks, this same "good" man is likened to Pilate keeping his hands clean.

The dramatic parody on the New Testament continues, shifting now from the Sermon on the Mount to Paul. A second trio appears: John Truman, the man with ledger, which may, like the Bible itself, be "the true book,"[36] who sells stock in the Black Rapids Coal Company, suggestive of hell, and in the New Jerusalem, with its fountain and lignum vitae suggestive of the heaven envisioned by John; the herb doctor, who is said to follow the profession of the

[34] *The Confidence-Man*, pp. 55, 54.
[35] *Ibid.*, p. 59.
[36] *Ibid.*, p. 73.

ancient herb doctor Solomon and who hawks the Samaritan Pain-Dissuader and advises customers to " 'Prove all the vials; trust those which are true' ";[37] and the man from the Philosophical Intelligence Office, with the brass plate, who advocates a more generous view of human nature. They represent faith, hope, and charity in the Pauline passage with which the book opens and which is reintroduced at the end of the first or Matthean trio when the woman in the ladies' saloon is discovered with her finger marking this passage in her gilt Testament.[38]

The architecture of *The Confidence-Man* is indeed formal. For although the Cosmopolitan, Frank Goodman, the last embodiment of the type, also seems to represent charity, he stands rather outside the two central trios, a conclusion to the whole as the deaf-mute was an introduction. His character, unlike those of his predecessors, is described in terms not of the New or the Old Testament but of the Apocrypha. Christian love is the disguise of all, expediency is their true nature, but for the first time this nature is presented directly, by comparison with the wisdom of the Hebrew sages, rather than by contrast. The irony, however, is sustained. For though the Confidence-Man in all his forms constantly quotes the New Testament, he is not familiar with the Old Testament and has never heard of the Apocrypha, the Scripture which perfectly describes him.

The penetration of the masquerade in this last episode, which is devoted to the task, is deliberate and thorough. In the character of Goodman the Confidence-Man converses

[37] *Ibid.*, p. 109.

[38] Miss Elizabeth Foster (*op. cit.*) is the discoverer of the principal Biblical allusions cited in these two paragraphs: the allusions to the Beatitudes in the characters of Black Guinea, Ringman, and the man with the gray coat, and to the Pauline virtues in the characters of Truman, the herb doctor, and the man from the P. I. O. For her permission to mention them here, and for her generous discussion with me of her whole interpretation of *The Confidence-Man*, I am deeply grateful. This interpretation will appear in her Introduction and Notes to the forthcoming edition of the novel to be issued by Hendricks House.

with the following passengers of the *Fidèle:* Pitch, who is
called an Ishmael; Charles Noble, who quotes a eulogy
of the winepress which incorporates portions of Proverbs;
Mark Winsome, who is first to acquaint Goodman with
Ecclesiasticus; a beggar; Egbert, in whose story of China
Aster there are references to Job and Solomon; William
Cream, who also quotes Ecclesiasticus; the old man in the
cabin, in whose Bible Goodman at last reads the book of
Sirach's son for himself; a boy peddler. Every important
character he meets, except Pitch, thus alludes in some fash-
ion to the wisdom books.

The actual words which they recall are all from one
book, Ecclesiasticus, many of them marked in Melville's
Bible. And they are bitter words indeed. In support of his
tortuous argument about the irresponsibility of snakes, Winsome concludes: " 'Hence that significant passage in Scripture, "Who will pity the charmer that is bitten with a
serpent?" ' "[39] Cream, next to quote from the same book,
remembers that he once refused credit to a customer who de-
sired it: " 'Because, I recalled what the son of Sirach says in
the True Book: "An enemy speaketh sweetly with his lips";
and so I did what the son of Sirach advises in such cases:
"I believed not his many words." ' "[40] And, adds the barber
in answer to Goodman's surprise at the source of the quotation, there are more verses like it in Proverbs.

His curiosity thus aroused by two successive acquaint-
ances, Goodman takes the first opportunity to read Ecclesiasticus for himself. In the Bible belonging to the old man,
who likewise is ignorant of the Apocrypha, he finds:

" 'Believe not his many words—an enemy speaketh sweetly
with his lips'—. . . 'With much communication he will tempt
thee; he will smile upon thee, and speak thee fair, and say
What wantest thou? If thou be for his profit he will use thee;
he will make thee bear, and will not be sorry for it. Observe

[39] *The Confidence-Man,* p. 252.   [40] *Ibid.,* p. 314.

and take good heed. When thou hearest these things, awake in thy sleep.' "[41]

The passage, a patchwork of several verses, is nothing less than a description of the Confidence-Man himself, as an occupant of one of the near-by berths asserts. The unmasking of the masquerader is now complete. Goodman himself assists in the final details, though ostensibly continuing to play his role, for separating the passage he has just read from the rest of the Bible, he raises a doubt about its veracity: " '. . . look, sir, all this to the right is certain truth, and all this to the left is certain truth, but all I hold in my hand here is apocrypha.' "[42] But the effect of this action is to identify him the more clearly with that which he left holding. The words of his last quotation from Scripture, " ' "Jehovah shall be thy confidence," ' "[43] far from being the comforting words they seem to him and the old man, form part of one of the most utilitarian chapters in the book of Proverbs. And at the last, extinguishing the lamp with its horned altar and its robed, haloed man, Goodman eliminates the emblems not of all religion but of the Old and the New Testament. What remains is the Apocrypha, in the darkness of whose ethics he is quite at home.

But not all the wisdom of the Hebrew sages was a formula for this world. There was also an element of metaphysical speculation in it, which was exercised to account for the school historically. All wisdom was thought in the beginning to have been an attribute of Jehovah, which he shared with his creatures. So as the conception of him deepened, greater areas of wisdom were declared inaccessible to men and known only to Jehovah. "Canst thou by searching find out God?" inquired Zophar of Job. Melville bracketed both his question and his answer: "It is as

[41] *Ibid.*, pp. 322-323.   [42] *Ibid.*, p. 324.
[43] *Ibid.*, p. 334.

high as heaven; what canst thou do? deeper than hell; what canst thou know?"[44] Nature itself seems to be a part of this forbidden area, a mighty mystery which exists solely for its own sake and which must not be approached too intimately. Again the picture is best drawn by Job. Beyond this natural scene, as beyond a veil, exists the Deity: amoral, inexorable, unknowable. Compared to the human aspect of Hebrew wisdom, its divine aspect is negative indeed.

Through *Mardi, Moby-Dick,* and *Pierre* may be traced this theme of divine, hidden wisdom. In each of these books the hero seems determined to enter a realm forbidden to him. From it he is warned by numerous omens, not the least of which are echoes from the thought and even the words of the Hebrew sages, but beside the fierceness of his resolve they are poor words at best. His course, measured by the standards of wisdom, is not only unprofitable but dangerous. Yet in spite of these standards, perhaps even because of them, he must pursue it.

He must pursue it, in *Mardi* and *Moby-Dick,* in a setting which is itself part of the universal secret. Like the Hebrew sages, Babbalanja's old sage Bardianna has no illusions about the natural world. Paraphrasing a New Testament verse of Scripture, he opines that " 'if not against us, nature is not for us.' "[45] Book X of his *Ponderings* pictures the starry heavens above Mardi, thereby diminishing the Mardian world very much as Job's world is made insignificant by Jehovah's naming over the constellations. Regarding the mountain peak of Maramma, the site of man's most direct communication with Oro, he " 'asserts that the plain alone was intended for man; who should be content to dwell under the shade of its groves, though the roots thereof descend into the darkness of the earth.' "[46]

[44] Job 11:7, 8.
[45] *Mardi,* I, 244.
[46] *Ibid.,* II, 2.

No more than his master does Babbalanja look for a revelation of the mysteries of the universe. Though geology as well as astronomy awes him, as they awed Job, neither yields its secret or defines religion. Even at the peak of his spiritual experience, his vision on the island of Serenia, he is impressed most with the limits of his knowledge compared to the boundless heavens within heavens before him. His interrogation of his archangelic guide, "Why create the germs that sin and suffer, but to perish?" receives the answer:

"'That,' breathed my guide, 'is the last mystery which underlieth all the rest. Archangel may not fathom it; that makes of Oro the everlasting mystery he is; that to divulge, were to make equal to himself in knowledge all the souls that are; that mystery Oro guards; and none but him may know.'"[47]

The question and answer echo a passage in Esdras, profusely marked in Melville's Bible. The prophet is conversing with the Archangel Uriel, the burden of whose speech is that there is a wisdom of earth and one of heaven, each unintelligible to inhabitants of the other place. Like Babbalanja, Esdras finally ventures the question to which there can be no reply:

Then I answered and said, How, and when shall these things come to pass? wherefore are our years few and evil?

And he answered me, saying, Do not thou hasten above the most Highest: for thy haste is in vain to be above him, for thou hast much exceeded.[48]

Inscrutable as nature is to Bardianna and Babbalanja, it is even more cruelly so to Ishmael. It is ambiguous as the color white; it masquerades in bright hues; it hides behind a mask. Moreover, when invaded by man it is actively hostile. Whatever the white whale symbolizes in

[47] *Ibid.*, II, 376.
[48] II Esdras 4:33-34.

the moral realm, it is something which can be avoided; men
need not encounter it. It is Ahab who pursues Moby-Dick,
as Starbuck perceives; at no time does the whale seek Ahab.
A subtle balance exists between the elements of creation,
and disaster ensues to the creature who destroys it. Even
the horse will throw its rider, as Job observed. Viewing
the skeleton of the dead whale, Ishmael recalls other words
of the same writer, words which Melville had penciled as
he read:

Is this the creature of whom it was once so triumphantly said—
"Canst thou fill his skin with barbed irons? or his head with fish-
spears? The sword of him that layeth at him cannot hold, the
spear, the dart, nor the habergeon: he esteemeth iron as straw;
the arrow cannot make him flee; darts are counted as stubble;
he laugheth at the shaking of a spear!"[49]

Merely to write of the gigantic creature of the deep fills
Ishmael with fear: "What am I that I should essay to hook
the nose of this leviathan! The awful tauntings in Job
might well appal me. 'Will he (the leviathan) make a
covenant with thee? Behold the hope of him is vain!' "[50]

Pierre also seems to invade forbidden territory, like Ahab
and like Taji. In his story the scene is undisguisedly moral,
and there is no natural phenomenon as there is in Job and in
Melville's other books to represent the alien character of
the realm he aspires to enter. But it is more clearly than
ever an unhuman, divine world. Pierre is Father Mapple's
true "patriot to heaven." And the course of action from
which he is warned is none other than that pursued by
Jesus, whom the New Testament represents as the Wisdom
of God.

Now this is the final development of the thought of the
Hebrew sages. Whereas their conception of wisdom was
first of a mystery, it is last of a revelation, an intermediary

[49] *Moby-Dick*, II, 94.
[50] *Ibid.*, I, 166-167.

force, bringing the nature of God to man. Ventured long after Job, this idea was instantly taken up and transformed by the early Christian theologians; and as it was adapted finally to the life of Jesus by Paul, it represented the Son as the incarnation of the Father's Wisdom. In fact, this very Pauline doctrine is quoted by Plinlimmon, in a passage dealing with "our so-called wisdom": "'Did He not expressly say—My wisdom (time) is not of this world? But whatever is really peculiar in the wisdom of Christ seems precisely the same folly to-day as it did 1850 years ago.' "[51] The pamphleteer errs, however, in attributing the words to Jesus himself. Marked in Melville's New Testament, they occur in Paul's first letter to the Corinthians, in the midst of his lengthiest and most famous exposition of divine wisdom.

It is for this reason that Pierre's fate is crueler than Ahab's or than Job's, because he is cut down in the act of revealing what at length has been ordained to remain no longer a mystery. But his fate, and Billy Budd's, is by no means unique. It is like that of the prophets and holy men lamented in Chronicles, Jeremiah, Proverbs, Baruch, and Ecclesiasticus: men infused with the spirit of wisdom but persecuted by the world. Jesus himself mourned them, supposedly quoting from a wisdom source: "O Jerusalem, Jerusalem, which killest the prophets, and stonest them that are sent unto thee; how often would I have gathered thy children together, as a hen doth gather her brood under her wings, and ye would not!"[52] Both this verse and the next, as well as the corresponding verses in Matthew, are marked in Melville's New Testament.

There can be no doubt that Melville knew this wisdom doctrine. He had read Ecclesiasticus and the Wisdom of Solomon, where its origins lay, and though the verses he marked in the former book do not include the great pas-

[51] *Pierre*, p. 295.
[52] Luke 13:34. See also Matt. 23:37.

sages on wisdom, he perspicaciously noted all the distinctive ideas in the latter. Indeed, in proportion to the number of verses in each book, the Wisdom of Solomon received more marks of Melville's pencil than any other in the Bible: one for every ninth verse. But Melville never traveled this last lap of the journey with the Hebrew sages. He never acquiesced in their belief that the emanant wisdom of God was not only a creative but a redemptive principle, seeking man to save him. He was not, for all his interest in mysticism, a true mystic; and he never lost himself in his essentially realistic universe.

On the contrary, not only in *Pierre* but in all his narratives the wisdom of the earth and the wisdom of heaven touch only to fly apart. They are two separate and unrelated systems for two dissimilar worlds. From *Typee* and *Omoo,* where the theory and practice of the missionaries are contrasted, through Redburn's attempt to reconcile the Liverpool docks and the New Testament, to White Jacket's conclusion "that although our blessed Saviour was full of the wisdom of heaven, yet His gospel seems lacking in the practical wisdom of earth,"[53] and from White Jacket to Mortmain, reasoning that Jesus's inability to descend from the cross proved true knowledge "'impotent for earth,'"[54] the contrast is the same.

More than a contrast, it is a feud. In *Mardi, Moby-Dick, Pierre,* and *The Confidence-Man* the worldly and unworldly systems of thought are not merely unrelated; each is madness to the other. After his conversion Babbalanja exclaims, "'I have been mad.'"[55] To the other members of his crew Ahab seems possessed, and Pip, cast into the depths of the sea, has its secrets revealed to him by "the miser-merman, Wisdom":

[53] *White Jacket,* p. 408.
[54] *Clarel,* II, 135.
[55] *Mardi,* II, 371.

He saw God's foot upon the treadle of the loom, and spoke it; and therefore his shipmates called him mad. So man's insanity is heaven's sense; and wandering from all mortal reason, man comes at last to that celestial thought, which, to reason, is absurd and frantic; and weal or woe, feels then uncompromised, indifferent as his God.[56]

Pierre, too, appears mad to his contemporaries. Despite the fact that he is briefly identified with Jesus, the Wisdom of God, his life is not the reconciliation which that life was, but a continual antagonism. It is a distortion of the source reminiscent of Father Mapple's omission from his sermon of Jehovah's pardon of the Ninevites. For it is to Paul's ironic "foolishness" that is "wisdom" that Melville alludes, not to the culminating vision of the Hebrew wise men which he marked in his Bible:

And being but one, she can do all things: and remaining in herself, she maketh all things new: and in all ages entering into holy souls, she maketh them friends of God, and prophets.

For God loveth none but him that dwelleth with wisdom.

For she is more beautiful than the sun, and above all the order of stars; being compared with the light, she is found before it.

For after this cometh night: but vice shall not prevail against wisdom.[57]

So in *The Confidence-Man,* where Goodman thinks it "Madness, to be mad,"[58] or excessively emotional, about anything, it is only the bitterest sentiments of Ecclesiasticus which are quoted, without an echo of Wisdom's lyrical consolation: "Come unto me, all ye that be desirous of me, and fill yourselves with my fruits."[59]

Much nearer this redemption and consolation surmounting Hebrew wisdom is the story of Billy Budd, who, with hardly "any trace of the wisdom of the serpent, nor yet

[56] *Moby-Dick,* II, 169-170.   [57] Wisd. of Sol. 7:27-30.
[58] *The Confidence-Man,* p. 232.   [59] Ecclus. 24:19.

quite a dove,"[60] is another victim of the feud between heaven and earth. But if this is a source for the tale, it is nowhere explicit. Billy's composure is the unshakable self-confidence of Taji, Ahab, and Pierre, now relieved of frenzy, transformed into peace.

III

Like the wisdom of the Old Testament, the theme of the Gospels pervades Melville's thought. It is strictly the theme of their moral rather than their religious code, however, for to Melville, as to most modern readers, this code was their great message. Significantly, most of the passages marked in his New Testament pertain to it. Jesus's other message, addressed to man as an individual soul who must know and obey God, who must create a new dispensation in himself rather than a new organization of society, Melville never seems to have recognized. And the presence of two such different principles in the life of one man appears not to have struck him at all.

On the single, ethical aspect of the Gospels, however, he heaped a double measure of admiration. Like all other attempts to rebuild the world closer to the heart's desire, it captivated him all his life, and both artistically and dialectically he touched upon it in every book from *Typee* to *Billy Budd*. In *Mardi* it was a major motif, and for *Pierre* it furnished the plot itself.

The tone in which Melville was always to speak of this theme is set in *Typee*, with his first mention of " 'the divine and gentle Jesus.' "[61] His constant adjectives to describe the Gospels are "meek" and "mild"; Jesus is "beautiful" and "genial," best represented by the "soft, curled, hermaphroditical Italian pictures."[62] The picture is the romantic one of Renan; of Sabatier, who was re-creating St. Francis of

---

[60] *Billy Budd and Other Prose Pieces*, p. 16.
[61] *Typee*, p. 273.
[62] *Moby-Dick*, II, 119.

Assisi along the same lines; of Saint-Évremond, author of a
sentence Melville copied on a flyleaf of his New Testament:
"Who well considers the Christian religion, would think
that God meant to keep it in the dark from our under-
standings, and make it turn upon the motions of our
hearts"; of Joubert, whose words, quoted by Arnold, Melville marked in his copy of Arnold's *Essays:* " 'The Old
Testament teaches the knowledge of good and evil; the
Gospel, on the other hand, seems written for the predesti-
nated; it is the book of innocence. The one is made for
earth, the other seems made for heaven.' " *Clarel* is full of
such images:

> "To Moses' law they [the Jews] yet did cling,
> But some would fain have tempering—
> In the bare place a bit of green.
> And lo, an advent—the Essene,
> Gentle and holy, meek, retired,
> With virgin charity inspired:
> Precursor, nay, a pledge, agree,
> Of light to break from Galilee.
> And, ay, He comes: the lilies blow!
> In hamlet, field, and on the road,
> To every man, in every mode
> How did the crowning Teacher show
> His broad and blessed comity.
> I do avow He still doth seem
> Pontiff of optimists supreme!"[63]

The words which Melville used to describe the Gospels
are, in fact, the same which he applied to the sanctuary
of the shore, the fertility of the field, the fixity of the isle,
the fellowship of society. They are his words, too, for describing Eden when it is employed as a symbol for man's
life of innocence before the fall. If, indeed, his imagery
is an indication of his deeper thought, it is apparent from

[63] *Clarel*, II, 30-31.

the first to the last of Melville's narratives that he never viewed the Gospel message as any part of the final truth. It is as the country is to Pierre, as the lee shore is to Bulkington, as the island of Serenia is to Taji. It is tempered to what Ishmael calls "green youth" in contrast to hoary and disillusioned old age, typified by Pierre's kinsman, who lives in the city and reads the Old Testament. In fact, Derwent speaking to Rolfe refers to "Green Christianity in glade."[64] It offers escape to all those who would linger fearfully in its arms. But all intrepid spirits must press on into what were to Melville greater complexities of thought and experience. True, in contrast to such abstract and often autocratic theorizing as that of Emerson, Melville found the Sermon on the Mount full of realism and compassion.[65] But in themselves the Gospels remained for him the record of a simple life. Sensitive as he was to all conflicts of the spirit, he never seemed to perceive those involved in the personal practice of Christian ethics.

Not only the dulcet and subordinate tone of Melville's Gospel theme is sounded in *Typee,* but the contrast with reality which was always to accompany it is also introduced. Wherever Melville looked about him he saw a discrepancy between the precepts of the New Testament and the practices of the world, a discrepancy he never, for all his disillusion, ceased protesting. His objection began with his reports on the missionaries and ended with the execution of Billy Budd.

Since as early as *Mardi* Melville so sweepingly rejected these same Gospels as final authority, such concern with

[64] *Ibid.,* I, 255.

[65] Beside the quotation from Emerson, "the calamity is the masses," in his copy of Alger's *Solitudes,* Melville noted: "These expressions attributed to the 'kindly Emerson' are somewhat different from the words of Christ to the multitude on the Mount." In his copy of Emerson's *Essays,* in answer to the notion that man sees only the evil which is in himself, he wrote: "But what did Christ see?—He saw what made him weep. . . . To annihilate all this nonsense read the Sermon on the Mount, and consider what it implies." (Melville's copies of both books are in the Harvard College Library.)

their immediate practicality seems unrealistic. But quite apart from their beguiling charm, which gave them a resemblance to the paradise of Eden, they had the single, uncompromising quality which was for him the hallmark of truth. And always there was about them, as there was not about Eden, the challenge of an ideal as yet unfulfilled. Melville could thus lament the failure of men to obey the Sermon on the Mount while at the same time, in a complex attitude, he urged all his heroes beyond it into uncharted seas.

It is *Mardi* in which the Gospel theme in this complexity is broached. Not only do Taji and his companions visit the island of organized religion, Maramma, but an ideal Christian society, Serenia, as well. For to Melville the ethic of Jesus was always a communal, not a personal, ideal. The prophet whose teachings are obeyed on Serenia is Alma, and with the word the benevolent atmosphere of the Gospels is once more suggested. The difference between the two islands, as one might expect from almost any writer, is altogether ethical. The Serenians practice what they preach, the Marammians do not. There is no doctrine or philosophy involved.

And this difference is what converts Babbalanja, who begins the voyage with Taji as a confirmed disbeliever in the religion of Alma. His objection to it is pragmatic: he has never seen it work. And ironically he is most skeptical on the island of Maramma, expressing his feeling to Mohi:

"For one, then, I wholly reject your Alma; not so much because of all that is hard to be understood in his histories; as because of obvious and undeniable things all round us; which, to me, seem at war with an unreserved faith in his doctrines as promulgated here in Maramma. Besides, everything in this isle strengthens my incredulity; I never was so thorough a disbeliever as now."[66]

[66] *Mardi*, II, 32.

Naturally, then, Babbalanja's discovery of Serenia has the immediate effect of converting him. Carried away with enthusiasm at the integrity of its inhabitants, he abandons Taji's party to remain forever among them. According to his own version of the incident, he becomes a convert to Alma himself, but it would be more precise to say he is won by the demonstration of a system's practicality. There is nothing personal in the experience; it does not touch the core of his being; it is not part of his effort to discover

"the essence of things; the mystery that lieth beyond; the elements of the tear which much laughter provoketh; that which is beneath the seeming; the precious pearl within the shaggy oyster. I probe the circle's centre; I seek to evolve the inscrutable."[67]

It is not revealed. For when Media suggests, in the midst of Maramma, that possibly those islanders have misconceived Alma's doctrine and Babbalanja should judge it on less circumstantial evidence, the philosopher replies: "'I know nothing more than that such is the belief in this land. And in these matters I know not where else to go for information.'"[68]

It is doubtless significant that old Bardianna's last will and testament is read before the party reaches Serenia, and thus Babbalanja has put behind him the wisdom of the sages in order to land on Alma's island. But Babbalanja remains a rationalist to the end, rejoicing to find that even on Serenia "'Reason no longer domineers; but still doth speak.'"[69] Even the vision he receives at his conversion is calculated to convince him of the superficiality of human knowledge, and the answer he hears to his inquiry regarding evil is the old answer of the wisdom books.

It is rather astonishing, indeed, to see how easily the skeptical Babbalanja is satisfied with this evasion, and to

[67] *Ibid.*, II, 36.   [68] *Ibid.*, II, 34.
[69] *Ibid.*, II, 371.

see further that the problem of evil, which conceivably might have deterred him from accepting Alma, does not enter his religious thought. He is vastly more perturbed by the inconsistencies of men than of God. And despite his perception of the effulgent "Shekinah" at the height of his dream, Babbalanja withdraws again into himself, concluding to Taji: " 'Within our hearts is all we seek: though in that search many need a prompter. Him I have found in blessed Alma.' "[70]

Serenia, in fact, is not the ultimate but the penultimate. More important than the differences between it and Maramma is the fact that neither harbors the maiden Yillah. She is not to be found in all Mardi. It is the sea, not the land, which gave her birth and which receives her again; even the sands of Alma's kingdom are as scorching to her as the shores of New England to Bulkington. But rather than venture after her into the unknown Babbalanja abandons the pursuit. For the elusive, final Yillah he substitutes the best Mardi has to offer, exclaiming to Taji:

"My voyage is ended. Not because what we sought is found; but that I now possess all which may be had of what I sought in Mardi. Here, I tarry to grow wiser still:—then I am Alma's and the world's. Taji! for Yillah thou wilt hunt in vain; she is a phantom that but mocks thee; and while for her thou madly huntest, the sin thou didst cries out, and its avengers still will follow. But here they may not come: nor those, who, tempting, track thy path. . . .

"Once more: Taji! be sure thy Yillah never will be found; or found, will not avail thee. Yet search, if so thou wilt; more isles, thou sayst, are still unvisited; and when all is seen, return, and find thy Yillah here."[71]

Babbalanja thus holds out Serenia to Taji not only as a substitute for Yillah but as a place of escape, where he will

[70] *Ibid.*, II, 380.
[71] *Ibid.*, II, 380-381.

be safe from his pursuers. But such an alternative the unsatisfied Taji spurns, and plunging into an "endless sea" still seeks the enigmatical nymph.

To Media also Serenia represents escape. For if the island does not hold the ultimate truth, neither does it offer a solution for the affairs of the world. Its way of life is ideal but not redemptive. Returning to Odo at last, with Babbalanja's suggestion that he introduce the religion of the Serenians abroad, Media finds his kingdom in the throes of a revolution. Presumably Alma can do nothing to save it. Forthwith the King sends Mohi and Yoomy back to Serenia, where they may be beyond danger, but as for himself, the valiant Media scorns the island's protection. He belongs to the great company of noble but doomed characters in Melville's narratives, whose funeral oration was delivered by Father Mapple. He will not compromise or flee, even to the bowers of Alma's island kingdom:

"Oh, friends! after our long companionship, hard to part! But henceforth, for many moons, Oro will prove no home for old age, or youth. In Serenia only, will ye find the peace ye seek; and thither ye must carry Taji, who else must soon be slain, or lost. Go: release him from the thrall of Hautia. Outfly the avengers, and gain Serenia. Reck not of me. The state is tossed in storms; and where I stand, the combing billows must break over. But among all noble souls, in tempest-time, the headmost man last flies the wreck. So, here in Oro will I abide, though every plank breaks up beneath me. And then,— great Oro! let the king die clinging to the keel! Farewell!"[72]

In *Pierre* the theme of the gospel ethics is resumed, and the atmosphere of Serenia is matched by that in the Glendinning home at Saddle Meadows. Pierre is a boy reared in an orthodox family, who, along with the forests and farms of his ancestors and

[72] *Ibid.*, II, 399.

by the same insensible sliding process . . . seemed to have in-
herited their docile homage to a venerable Faith, which the first
Glendinning had brought over sea, from beneath the shadow
of an English minster. Thus in Pierre was the complete pol-
ished steel of the gentleman, girded with Religion's silken
sash. . . .[73]

It was his father's belief that all claims to manhood were
empty unless "the primeval gentleness and golden humanities of religion had been so thoroughly wrought into the
complete texture of the character, that he who pronounced
himself gentleman, could also rightfully assume the meek,
but kingly style of Christian."[74] That this "meek religion
is of the New rather than the Old Testament is made clear
by the allusion to the shrine Pierre has erected in his heart
to his father, "spotless, and still new as the marble of the
tomb of him of Arimathea,"[75] and by the description of
grandfather Glendinning's portrait: "a glorious gospel
framed and hung upon the wall, and declaring to all people,
as from the Mount, that man is a noble, godlike being, full
of choicest juices; made up of strength and beauty."[76]

In the same light, at the beginning of the book, Pierre
views Isabel, who, despite her isolated childhood has acquired the conventional religious vocabulary. In her first
letter to him she declares: " 'No more, oh no more, dear
Pierre, can I endure to be an outcast in the world, for
which the dear Saviour died.' "[77] And at his first sight of
her Pierre is impressed by her spirituality: "Out from the
infantile, yet eternal mournfulness of the face of Isabel,
there looked on Pierre that angelic childlikeness, which our
Saviour hints is the one only investiture of translated souls;
for of such—even of little children—is the other world."[78]

The picture of the Gospels in *Pierre,* then, is not different
from that in *Mardi.* Pierre's story begins where Taji's

[73] *Pierre,* p. 6.   [74] *Ibid.*
[75] *Ibid.,* p. 95.   [76] *Ibid.,* p. 40.
[77] *Ibid.,* p. 88.   [78] *Ibid.,* p. 198.

leaves off: with the best the world has to offer the aspiring spirit. But Melville's handling of the theme here is complicated by the fact that, Saddle Meadows being no Serenia, Pierre becomes temporarily involved in an effort to practice the precepts of Christianity in a hostile environment. Actually this is not his primary aim. Pierre never opposes virtue to vice, but the singleness of his vision and his will to the ambiguities of society, his *virtù* to disaster. And eventually, like Taji, he is impelled beyond even the idealism of the Gospels in his pursuit of certainty. For the symbol of his goal, Isabel, is as utterly outside the sphere of conventional experience as Yillah or as Moby-Dick. It is Lucy rather who is affiliated with Saddle Meadows by an "angelic childlikeness."

This preliminary theme, however, of the difference between Christian doctrine and behavior, is elaborated at such length as almost to obscure the major theme of the ultimate inadequacy of both. Nowhere else does Melville spend so much time motivating his hero's grand quest. The shorelessness of Yillah and of Moby-Dick is merely predicated, but Isabel's is argued, and that by a not altogether logical allegory. To embrace her Pierre must leave the haven of Saddle Meadows because there she divides opinion; there the wisdom of heaven defends and the wisdom of earth repudiates her. That the equivalent of heavenly wisdom in this scheme, the ethics of the Gospels, should in the end prove less than absolute confuses the Biblical motifs throughout the book. On the other hand, the fact that two of the spokesmen of earthly wisdom, Pierre's kinsman and Plinlimmon, live in the city and that Pierre's perusal of the New Testament does not extend beyond the country scenes of the book lends structural support to Melville's primary thesis: the Gospels belong to the idyllic period of man's innocence.

The idea of reconciling these two wisdoms, which occurs to neither Ahab nor Taji nor the Serenians themselves,

Pierre takes from the bold example of Jesus, with whom he momentarily becomes identified. But, even so, he is fore-doomed to failure. No more than in *Mardi* can the social enterprise of the Gospels be carried on in the world's midst. The difference between heaven and earth is still unsur-mountable, ineradicable, irreconcilable—a difference which is the burden here of Plinlimmon's pamphlet.

This flimsy rag in *Pierre* corresponds architecturally to Father Mapple's sermon in *Moby-Dick*. Each is a précis of the plot. The setting, too, in which the message is de-livered is again symbolic. For Pierre reads Plinlimmon in the coach, as he is halfway between Saddle Meadows and the city, between the idealism of his youth and the bitter truth of advancing years, between the contemplation of "that greatest real miracle of all religions, the Sermon on the Mount" and of mammonish society all about. The con-trast in Pierre's mind between the Gospels and the world continues:

From that divine mount, to all earnest loving youths, flows an inexhaustible soul-melting stream of tenderness and loving-kindness; and they leap exulting to their feet, to think that the founder of their holy religion gave utterance to sentences so infinitely sweet and soothing as these; sentences which embody all the love of the Past, and all the love which can be imagined in any conceivable Future. Such emotions as that sermon raises in the enthusiastic heart; such emotions all youthful hearts refuse to ascribe to humanity as their origin. This is of God! cries the heart, and in that cry ceases all inquisition. Now, with this fresh-read sermon in his soul, the youth again gazes abroad upon the world. Instantly, in aggravation of the former sole-cism, an overpowering sense of the world's downright positive falsity comes over him; the world seems to lie saturated and soaking with lies. . . .

Hereupon then in the soul of the enthusiast youth two armies come to the shock; and unless he prove recreant, or unless he prove gullible, or unless he can find the talismanic secret, to reconcile this world with his own soul, then there is no peace for him, no slightest truce for him in this life.[79]

But of course there is no such talismanic secret, as Melville hastens to add; there are only the partial solutions offered by such philosophers and speculators as Plinlimmon, in his symbolically fragmentary pamphlet: its conclusion, in Pierre's tattered copy, torn away, its gaps in thought filled by asterisks. This eccentric, whom Pierre later meets in the city, here pictures the moral systems of heaven and of earth as two systems of time, for which two timekeeping devices are necessary. Jesus, according to him, was the only perfect chronometer; his followers, of whom Pierre is typical, not only are imperfect but in their attempt to abide by celestial time upon the earth array all worldly timekeepers against them and incur misfortune and death. The somewhat irrelevant distinction drawn is that although Jesus encountered death, he was never, like them, guilty of folly or sin. It almost seems, in fact, that Plinlimmon passes too lightly over the fact that Jesus died, too. For if the two times are intrinsically incompatible, death is the expected lot of every chronometer, whatever its degree of perfection. Despite his free thinking, the philosopher seems still to be bound by the doctrinal view of Jesus's character.

The solution which Plinlimmon offers, as might be expected, is a virtuous expediency. Identifying the injunctions to turn the left cheek and to bestow everything on the poor as chronometrical, he assures his readers that all that can be required of a man, an horologe, is to give alms moderately and to abstain from downright evil. The whole history of Christendom since the death of its founder but convinces him that

"the only great original moral doctrine of Christianity (*i.e.* the chronometrical gratuitous return of good for evil, as distin-

[79] *Ibid.*, pp. 289-290.

,guished from the horological forgiveness of injuries taught by some of the Pagan philosophers), has been found (horologically) a false one. . . ."[80]

With this pragmatic conclusion of Plinlimmon the wisdom theme disappears from Pierre, leaving the theme of the Gospels themselves more distinct. That, even considered absolutely, they are inadequate to Pierre's needs is apparent in this same carriage scene. For finding himself beset with doubt, Pierre exorcises it by appealing not to Scripture but to the chivalry of his own action. Even his Christlike attitude to Isabel is insufficient for the hour of passion and incest which soon follows their arrival in the city. Replacing the dominant image of the Sermon on the Mount at the first of the book is the dream of Enceladus the Titan at the last. With the geographical transition, in fact, all Biblical motifs disappear from his story, while Pierre's pursuit of the absolute goes the more furiously forward.

For once more Melville's hero, renouncing all for his dream, renounces also religion. Behind him in rural Saddle Meadows Pierre leaves the Gospels, and indeed in the same words the two are constantly described: "the sweet fields of Saddle Meadows," "sentences so infinitely sweet and soothing." Both belong to the period of the " 'sweet docilities' " of his youth.[81] But the truth lies elsewhere. And Pierre fleeing to the seaport in search of the ultimate is like the familiar sailor of Melville's imagination, spurning the green shore:

Weary with the invariable earth, the restless sailor breaks from every enfolding arm, and puts to sea in height of tempest that blows off shore. But in long night-watches at the antipodes, how heavily that ocean gloom lies in vast bales upon the deck; thinking that that very moment in his deserted hamlet-home the household sun is high, and many a sun-eyed maiden

[80] *Ibid.*, p. 300.   [81] *Ibid.*, pp. 282, 289, 25.

meridian as the sun. He curses Fate; himself he curses; his senseless madness, which is himself. For whoso once has known this sweet knowledge, and then fled it; in absence, to him the avenging dream will come.[82]

The magnitude of Pierre's "avenging dream" is a final testimony to the secondary nature of the Gospels in his thought. For though they motivated his great renunciation, the motivation of all Melville's characters is less important than their uncompromising action; and it fades into inconsequence beside the cataclysmic end of that action. The fate of Pierre, like that of Ahab, is out of all proportion to its original cause. There is no connection between his simple declaration of brotherly love to Isabel and the blindness, bankruptcy, incest, murder, and suicide in which he is finally involved. But this is the tragic fate of all relentless seekers of the truth. When Pierre passes beyond the externalities of ethics, even of the noble Sermon on the Mount, he forever gives up " 'quietly reaping in a Christian corn-field' " for " 'recklessly ploughing the waters of the most barbaric seas.' "[83]

From *The Confidence-Man* alone this wistfulness of the Gospel theme is largely absent. So bitterly ironic is its introduction, in the characters of Black Guinea, Ringman, the man with the gray coat, and all the sharpsters who glibly quote the charitable words of Paul, that it hardly appears as a serious way of life, even for one corner of the world. The contrast is not between its preaching and its practice but between the exploitation and the honest rejection of it. At first it seems that, as Plinlimmon perceived, the ethical code of Christianity is simply impractical, and that because of a fact which he largely ignored: the innate, ineradicable selfishness of human nature.

But this is not the sole reason for the mean appearance of the New Testament ethic in this novel. Not only the evil

[82] *Ibid.*, p. 252.   [83] *Moby-Dick*, I, 317.

of men, but the harshness of unhuman truth defies it. The wooden-legged, gimlet-eyed pessimist draws a sharper distinction than Plinlimmon when he cries,

"Charity is one thing, and truth is another. . . .
"To where it belongs with your charity! to heaven with it!
. . . here on earth, true charity dotes, and false charity plots."[84]

His sentiment is echoed by the merchant, Roberts, who is moved by the story of Goneril to query:

". . . can wine or confidence percolate down through all the stony strata of hard considerations, and drop warmly and ruddily into the cold cave of truth? Truth will *not* be comforted. Led by dear charity, lured by sweet hope, fond fancy essays this feat; but in vain; mere dreams and ideals, they explode in your hand, leaving naught but the scorching behind!"[85]

This being so, the message of the Gospels and of Paul is worse than impractical; it is a deceiving and a misleading message, precisely as it is in the hands of the Confidence-Man. And this is why such characters as Pitch and Moredock, more single-minded than he, reject it altogether, even at the cost of being branded as misanthropes. In this narrative, in fact, the role of Taji and of Pierre is played by Moredock: the unsatisfied idealist, renouncing religion along with other solaces, spurning society though not hating mankind, or rather loving men by hating them.

Yet even in *The Confidence-Man* a vestige of the old sweetness of the gospel theme remains. Moredock is not an Indian-hater par excellence. Periodically he is drawn back from his desperate purpose by the " ' "Soft enticements of domestic life." ' "[86] And for their part, it is from this same Eden of felicity that the Indians are driven by him. For his presence penetrates their forests "like the voice calling through the garden."[87]

<hr>

[84] *The Confidence-Man*, pp. 15-16.   [85] *Ibid.*, p. 87.
[86] *Ibid.*, p. 201.   [87] *Ibid.*, p. 205.

IV

All the while contained in these same Gospels whose ethics Melville continued to admire and reject was another theme which, for its greater realism, came to have deeper and deeper meaning for him, and which he never associated with the visionary Sermon on the Mount at all. It was the instinctive and irreconcilable conflict of good and evil, which in the New Testament issued in the crucifixion of Jesus. This is the theme of *Billy Budd*. In fact, although here alone it is presented by means of the Biblical allegory, this is to some extent the theme in all Melville's novels. His images for the conflict are numerous: the Vermont colt snorting at the buffalo robe, the hostility of blond and brunet, the Zoroastrian antithesis of light and darkness. Most appropriately of all he represented it as an exchange of physical fisticuffs between two men.

The central incident in *Billy Budd* is, indeed, an old story refurbished with new names. Claggart is another Jackson, the bully of the *Highlander;* and Budd is Captain Jack Chase of the *Neversink,* whose crew also contains a forerunner of Claggart in the person of the smuggler Bland. Bland occupies the same post as Claggart on board ship, master-at-arms, and he too is characterized by a peculiar natural depravity. He is "an organic and irreclaimable scoundrel, who did wicked deeds as the cattle browse the herbage, because wicked deeds seemed the legitimate operation of his whole infernal organisation."[88]

The symbolism of color is added to the clash in *Moby-Dick,* with the pairing off of Daggoo and the Spanish sailor, the opposition of black and white within "the ringed horizon."[89] The contrast is repeated in *Billy Budd,* when the blond Budd faces the black-haired Claggart.

With *Moby-Dick,* too, Melville seems to have begun thinking of the conflict of good and evil in terms of its

[88] *White Jacket,* p. 234.   [89] *Moby-Dick,* I, 221.

great Biblical version, the Crucifixion. The instance occurs
in the episode of the *Town-Ho*. According to Ishmael, the
feud between Steelkilt and Radney is the result of their
instinctive personal antipathy for each other. In the ensuing action Steelkilt is the nonaggressor, Radney is not so
much evil as "doomed and made mad," and an inscrutable
fate presides over the affairs of both.

When Steelkilt is betrayed to his captain by his two
fellow-mutineers, all three are hung up in the mizzen rig-
ging until morning. At dawn, in the presence of all the
crew, he flogs them where they hang before cutting them
down. The scene is an inescapable reminder of Billy
Budd's sunrise hanging. Indeed, in this position the innocent Steelkilt and his traitorous companions bring to Melville's mind the image of Jesus hanging between the two
malefactors: " " ". . . seizing a rope, he [the captain] applied
it with all his might to the backs of the two traitors, till
they yelled no more, but lifelessly hung their heads side-
ways, as the two crucified thieves are drawn." ' "⁹⁰

And since the story of Jesus's death is thus already connected with the episode, it seems likely, from a subsequent
phrase, that Melville also associated the betrayal of Steelkilt by his friends with the betrayal of Jesus. Planning to
take his revenge during a night watch when Radney dozes
on deck, Steelkilt " 'calculated his time, and found that his
next trick at the helm would come round at two o'clock,
in the morning of the third day from that in which he
had been betrayed.' "⁹¹ So far as Steelkilt's affairs are con-
cerned, the three days mean nothing, for in the interval
Moby-Dick destroys Radney. But in Jesus's life this is
the important period between the Crucifixion and the
Resurrection.

By the time of *White Jacket* a criminal suspended above
the deck of a ship seems to have been fixed in Melville's

⁹⁰ *Ibid.*, I, 322.   ⁹¹ *Ibid.*, I, 325.

mind as an image of the Crucifixion. Bland, the smuggling master-at-arms on the *Neversink,* and a spiritual duplicate of Claggart, deserves to be so hanged, but White Jacket continues to defend him: ". . . I will stand by even a man-of-war thief, and defend him from being seized up at the gangway, if I can—remembering that my Saviour once hung between two thieves, promising one life eternal. . . ."[92]

This passivity of Jesus's resistance, once the clash with evil has occurred, is also foreshadowed in Melville's depiction of character before *Billy Budd.* His nonresistance is at least as much naturalistic as religious in such characters as Pip, Bartleby, and Benito Cereno, but often it bears the seal of the New Testament. Jarl, Daniel Orme, and Agath are tattooed with the image of the Crucifixion; and Israel Potter becomes "the bescarred bearer of a cross"[93] when the cut he received at Bunker Hill is traversed by a cutlass wound in the encounter of the *Bon Homme Richard* and the *Serapis.* The figure is repeated in the eighth sketch of "The Encantadas," when Hunilla, the stoical Chola widow, is pictured "passing into Payta town, riding upon a small gray ass; and before her on the ass's shoulders, she eyed the jointed workings of the beast's armorial cross."[94]

When the theme of the Crucifixion is taken up finally in *Billy Budd,* the New Testament story is clearly visible. Fundamentally, of course, the two main characters in the novel are embodiments of two abstractions. In one sense Budd is simple nature, a barbarian, "Adam . . . ere the urbane Serpent wriggled himself into his company."[95] Yet his innocence is more than that of a natural man, completely unarmed in the world. It is a divine innocence, incorruptible by society or the forces of darkness. It is a communicable quality, too, to such an extent that Billy's captain on

[92] *White Jacket,* p. 234.
[93] *Israel Potter,* p. 222.
[94] *The Piazza Tales,* p. 235. See also *Clarel,* I, 177; II, 296.
[95] *Billy Budd and Other Prose Pieces,* pp. 16-17.

the *Rights of Man* says of him, as Jesus said of himself: "'Not that he preached to them or said or did anything in particular; but a virtue went out of him, sugaring the sour ones.'"[96]

The spiritual antithesis of Billy is Claggart, the master-at-arms, who represents "depravity according to nature." It is a quality not consisting of petty vices nor engendered by experience, but innately residing in his inmost being. He is not so much an evil man as an evil principle, described by such words as those in Proverbs 21:10, which Melville marked: "The soul of the wicked desireth evil. . . ." Admittedly Melville had some Biblical parallel in mind, for when he came to analyze Claggart he indulged in an illuminating digression. Recording a youthful conversation with a friend on the subject of penetrating character, he quoted the friend as saying:

"Coke and Blackstone hardly shed so much light into obscure spiritual places as the Hebrew prophets. And who were they? Mostly recluses."

At the time my inexperience was such that I did not quite see the drift of all this. It may be that I see it now. And, indeed, if that lexicon which is based on Holy Writ were any longer popular, one might with less difficulty define and denominate certain phenomenal men. As it is, one must turn to some authority not liable to the charge of being tinctured with the Biblical element.[97]

[96] *Ibid.*, p. 9.

[97] *Ibid.*, p. 45. This lexicon may be the celebrated work of Thomas Wilson, *A Complete Christian Dictionary*, printed in London in 1612 and by 1678 in its eighth edition. Wilson defined "Evil" thus: "The *devil* is evil, not in substance or person, but in nature or quality; Not by creation from God, by voluntary departure from God and goodness: Evil he is originally and perfectly, but not infinitely; to all eternity, but not from all eternity.

"The like we may say of evil men, except in their originality of evil." Of "Innocency" he wrote: "A meer voidness of fault, and freedom from all sin. In this estate Adam was created. This is perfect innocency by creation." (Quotations are from the eighth edition, augmented by Bagwell and Simson.) The two passages might well "define and denominate" both Claggart and Budd.

Yet while Billy and Claggart are essentially abstractions, arrayed against each other by their very natures, for the purposes of the plot they play the roles of Jesus and Judas. Though he is not a creature of the secondary or auxiliary nature of Judas, Claggart is as effective a betrayer of an innocent man to authority. His first attempt is by bribery: he has a seaman offer Billy two guineas to join a proposed mutiny group. When that temptation is withstood, Claggart falsely charges that Billy is disloyal to the king. Only in this way, by treachery, can evil reach good. So Jesus was betrayed by Judas after he had resisted the temptations of Satan in the wilderness, and above him on the cross was hung the same charge: treason.

Both these indictments, moreover, go unanswered. When Budd is brought into the cabin and hears Claggart's accusation he does not utter a word in self-defense, just as Jesus remained silent before the priests and elders. The experience has brought out his defect of speech and he is momentarily paralyzed, though making agonized efforts to speak and defend himself. Perceiving the situation, Vere offers him more time in which to reply, but he is not successful in soothing the sailor:

Contrary to the effect intended, these words, so fatherly in tone, doubtless touching Billy's heart to the quick, prompted yet more violent efforts at utterance—efforts soon ending for the time in confirming the paralysis, and bringing to the face an expression which was as a crucifixion to behold.[98]

Then comes Budd's response to Claggart's accusation, not consciously but instinctively. There can be no compromise between the two forces which they represent, and Claggart falls fatally under Budd's blow. Nor can there be compromise between what remains: between Budd and the king's statute, under which he is now subject to trial. It does not matter that in nature he is free; it does not matter

[98] *Billy Budd and Other Prose Pieces,* p. 73.

that in breaking an immediate law he thereby kept one higher. Nor does his intent enter into the case; he is judged solely by his deed. The purity of his conscience is reserved for consideration until the Last Assizes, where, as Vere remarks, it will surely acquit him. Here he is the double victim of malignity and of custom.

Thus poignantly and dramatically did Melville distinguish between the false and the true charge against Budd. The distinction is the same in the trial of Jesus. The charge of treason which the members of the Sanhedrin proffered, though necessary for his official execution, was not only false, it was superficial in their own minds. Their true grievance against him was the fact that in obeying the spirit of the law, even more faithfully than they, Jesus violated its letter. Under a similar primitive code both he and the Handsome Sailor are condemned: the Mosaic law and the Mutiny Act. The similarity between the two codes is not insignificant. For the Mutiny Act, demanding a life for a life, is in effect the same penalizing legalism as the Old Testament ethic—the same, in fact, which finally drove Pierre from Saddle Meadows.

Throughout these scenes Captain Vere stands in two relationships to Budd. Primarily he is the military superior and disciplinarian. He sacrifices everything to the end of having Billy convicted, calling a drumhead court together lest in the delay he be swayed by the essential right and wrong of the case from the execution of his duty as administrator of the drastic law. Like Pilate, he condemns to death a man whom he knows to be innocent, though unlike Pilate he accepts the full responsibility of his act. Melville may have known, too, that apocryphal story that Pilate was haunted by the memory of Jesus during his last years as praetor of Hispania Tarraconensis. Not far from this locality Vere murmurs Budd's name as he lies dying on Gibraltar.

Yet Vere also appears in the role of Billy's father; as Abraham to Isaac, as God to Jesus—or rather, not as Abraham to Isaac. Among numerous figures of speech emphasizing the general father-son relationship of the two men this one, brief as it is, provides a revealing contrast with the particular relationship which Melville was also at pains to establish between them. In the private interview between the foretopman and his captain before the execution Melville imagines:

The austere devotee of military duty, letting himself melt back into what remains primeval in our formalised humanity, may in the end have caught Billy to his heart, even as Abraham may have caught young Isaac on the brink of resolutely offering him up in obedience to the exacting behest.[99]

The figure is moving, but the parallel can be carried no further. For Isaac did not die. Even waiving the fact that his near sacrifice is a deliberate scheme of the Old Testament Jehovah, the obedience of Isaac and of Billy Budd are two different things. Isaac was not taken into Abraham's confidence any more than Abraham was taken into Jehovah's. All is blind obedience, dependent on a jealous and capricious deity.

Not so is the sympathy between Budd and Vere. The sailor and the officer meet as equals; neither conceals anything from the other. When confused at the trial Budd turns to Vere, his accuser, for counsel. His only concern is to have himself cleared in the mind of his captain, to be understood if not to understand; when that is accomplished he has no fear of the future. Their interview alone in Vere's cabin is not unlike the episode in Gethsemane. Afterward the foretopman possesses a peace marvelous and ineffable, which even the chaplain cannot fathom. As he goes to his death his last words are, " 'God bless Captain Vere!' "[100]

[99] *Ibid.*, pp. 91-92.   [100] *Ibid.*, p. 102.

It is from this understanding which exists between Budd and Vere that the tone of acceptance in *Billy Budd* derives its peculiar quality. It is not stoicism, nor the exhaustion following such intense but vain resistance as that of Ahab and of Pierre. It is not even the negation of Jesus's injunction to "resist not evil," which Melville marked in his New Testament. It is a singular mystic communion with the heart of the creation. These two meet on a plane which their companions do not touch or comprehend. They are in a peculiar sense one being. Each shares "in the rarer qualities of one nature—so rare, indeed, as to be all but incredible to average minds, however much cultivated. . . ."[101]

This role of Vere is, in fact, the chief addition Melville made in *Billy Budd* to his previous brief dramatizations of the great conflict of good and evil. In them there is no one corresponding to him, an administrator of the law who both knows and loves the law's victim, and in return is known and loved himself. Oro is inaccessible to Mardians, Ahab's fire spirit is disembodied, even Alma and the founder of Pierre's religion are but the instigators of a system, and the chaplain of the *Indomitable* is only a cog in that system. These characters cannot perceive the personality behind the mask, and therefore fear, defy, and blindly obey it. But Billy Budd sees Captain Vere face to face, and finds at the heart of creation the warmth of personality.

This is, of course, easily recognizable as a New Testament idea of the nature of the universe, presided over by a fatherly god. But Melville read something more than this into the Crucifixion story. There he found one more illustration for his notion that beyond the farthest known truth there is yet an untrodden realm, an undisclosed mystery. Unlike Jehovah in the Old Testament, God the Father seems to practice as well as to command obedience;

[101] *Ibid.*, p. 91.

hence his enigmatical willingness for Jesus to die. And so in *Billy Budd* even he who administers the law is bound by it. It is the fact that Vere did not formulate the Mutiny Act which makes possible the community of spirit between him and Billy Budd. Both are subject to a power beyond themselves.

What this power is, what this realm is in which, as in Hebrew wisdom, God himself does not reign, Melville never concluded. But it is clearly not simply evil. It is beyond good or evil; it is beyond conflict. The realm in which Budd meets Vere is not the same as that in which he meets Claggart, and beyond them all is an utterly amoral, mysteriously influential *terra incognita*. The last of all Melville's symbols, the death of Captain Vere in the encounter with the *Athéiste,* is a fitting one. Religion, even in its noblest aspect, remained for him penultimate.

The mystery in *Billy Budd* is thus not altogether one of iniquity. It is the mystery of a boundless creation, an infinite number of superficially exclusive, deeply related spheres. Symbolic of their existence and of their interdependence is the fact that all nature is affected at Budd's death, as it was at the death of Jesus; it is an episode comparable to Nehemiah's burial in *Clarel,* when a rainbow appears in the sky. The moral conflict is not confined to its own world but reaches beyond it, even to the unyielding elements. When Budd's body is hoisted aloft the violent motion usually noticeable at hangings is absent; it is suspended quietly above the heads of his comrades. At the same moment the appearance of the sea and sky becomes phenomenal:

. . . the vapoury fleece hanging low in the east, was shot through with a soft glory as of the fleece of the Lamb of God seen in mystical vision, and simultaneously therewith, watched by the wedged mass of upturned faces, Billy ascended; and ascending, took the full rose of the dawn.[102]

[102] *Ibid.,* p. 103.

It is not accidental that the description contains a suggestion of the Ascension and of the doctrine of the Atonement. For in the manuscript of *Billy Budd* the word "shekinah" is crossed out in favor of "rose," and at the beginning of the next chapter Melville first referred to Billy's "ascension" but changed it to his "execution."

Finally, when Billy's remains are lowered into the sea, throngs of birds fly screaming to the spot and circle it as the ship passes out of sight. And at last it is related that for several years the sailors of the *Indomitable* knew the whereabouts of the spar from which Billy was suspended, following it from ship to dockyard to ship again. "To them a chip of it was as a piece of the Cross."[103]

This subtle yet inescapable connection between the natural and supernatural worlds was always part of Melville's vision. If they could not be fitted into one system of thought and action, they were as impossible to separate as the past and the present. The mystery of their relationship never ceased to fascinate him. And though he found it impossible to resolve, he constantly made one distinction between these two parts of the universe. The invisible sphere is absolute, as the themes of Old Testament prophecy and of New Testament ethics and theology insist. But the vast scene which meets the eye, as the Hebrew sages also knew, is ambiguous, equivocal, disguised, relative, masked, multiple.

Nor at any point was this relationship between the visible and invisible fixed. It was perpetually shifting, continually to be recharted, like the *Pequod's* devious course. Time, as Melville and as the author of Ecclesiastes saw it, was the great exigency, bending both good and evil, both idea and reality. In the actual performance of his duty Captain Vere is bound more by the time at which he is called upon to judge Billy Budd than he is by the law it-

[103] *Ibid.*, p. 113.

self. For the episode on board the *Indomitable* occurs during a year of war and, more particularly, a few months after the great Nore Mutiny of 1797. Had the times been different, Budd might have received lenient treatment, or might not have been impressed into naval service in the first place. It is a qualification reminiscent of Father Mapple's warning to those who seek "to pour oil upon the waters when God has brewed them into a gale"; of King Media's failure to put Serenian precepts into practice in Odo because of the revolution sweeping the island; of Pierre's misfortune to be created a chronometer in a world of horologes. The figure, essentially the Preacher's conception of moral times and seasons, approaches the next century's vision of a dynamic fourth dimension.

For although his world is firmly objective, Melville's thought followed existential rather than logical lines. With dramatic sharpness he perceived that the manifestations of reality are relative, and that either end of life is nearer the undivided nature of truth. It is not without significance that the carpenter of the *Pequod* is described as being "uncompromised as a new-born babe,"[104] and that Pip feels "uncompromised" only when he is near to drowning in the vast and open sea.[105]

[104] *Moby-Dick*, II, 234.   [105] *Ibid.*, II, 170.

Style

IF MELVILLE'S THEMES and characters are few in number, his style, like his imagery, is astonishingly varied. Evidences of his reading may be found here even when they are absent from his content. For a study of certain literary techniques not his own was one of his serious interests, and his imitation of them is characteristic of his fondness for experiment. These imitations are not sustained, for the most part extending no farther than a short paragraph. They are responsible, however, for one of the chief characteristics of Melville's style—its overtones. It is a style enriched by rhythmical as well as imagistic associations, so that as the words are read the counterpoint of other words is audible.

Anglo-Saxon kennings, Elizabethan rhythms, Rabelaisian exaggerations, not to mention the words of little-known *voyageurs*—these are among the echoes in Melville's pages. Most widely dispersed of all, though of the same brief and experimental character, are echoes of the Bible: quotations and imitations of the King James Version, adaptations of the Hebrew literary tradition.

I

The amount of Melville's actual quotation from any of his sources is slight, and so it is with his use of Scripture.

About one sixth of his allusions may thus be classified. They come from about half the canonical and one of the apocryphal books, and in themselves represent the major variations in Biblical style. Most often represented is Matthew, from which there are two dozen quotations. Next come Isaiah, John, Corinthians, Psalms, Luke, and Genesis, a list according in general with the books most thoroughly marked in Melville's Bible and New Testament.

Of these excerpts, approximately seventy are acknowledged by the use of quotation marks, punctuation which detaches them somewhat from their context and gives them the nature of a commentary or an authority. A characteristic use of a verse thus quoted is as a motto, reminiscent of the mottoes of seventeenth-century emblems. Beneath the title of the poem "The Enthusiast" appears the line, *"Though He slay me yet will I trust in Him"*; beneath that of "The Buddha," *"For what is your life? It is even a vapour that appeareth for a little time and then vanisheth away"*; beneath the Epilogue of *Moby-Dick,* "And I only am escaped alone to tell thee." Five of the "Extracts" at the beginning of *Moby-Dick* are Biblical. The inscription on Merrymusk's tombstone is:

"O death, where is thy sting?
O grave, where is thy victory?"[1]

that on the tombstone of Clarel's friend: " ' "I KNOW THAT MY REDEEMER LIVETH." ' "[2] Ruth's tablecloth bears the woven exclamation, " 'IF I FORGET THEE, O JERUSALEM!' "[3]

Other direct quotations are more functional in Melville's narratives, which, as they unfold, are often dramatizations of these words. Bildad, Frank Goodman, and Nehemiah, who read aloud from the Bible, and Father Mapple, who preaches from it, thereby announce the themes of their

[1] *Billy Budd and Other Prose Pieces*, p. 172.
[2] *Clarel*, I, 155.
[3] *Ibid.*, I, 107.

own stories. Like a preacher himself taking his text, Melville put verses in their mouths upon which he then proceeded to write homilies. It would hardly be surprising to discover that he consciously assumed this role. For the number of actual sermons he referred to, summarized, and composed in his books is far larger than his orthodox background can account for. They could have come only from one inspired himself by the possibilities of texts and of preaching.

Far greater in number, however, than his direct and acknowledged quotations from the Bible are those which Melville incorporated without quotation marks and usually without reference to their source. Some of them appear numerous times, from his early to his last books, in widely different contexts. They are linguistic favorites of his, as he had certain favorites among the persons and events of the Bible in his imagery. Repeatedly he spoke of the injunctions to be as wise as serpents and as harmless as doves, to sell all one has, to take no thought for the morrow. He mentioned the valley of dry bones, death on a pale horse, the mystery of iniquity, the man of sorrows, the many mansions of heaven. He reiterated that life is but a vapor, that in the millennium the lion will lie down with the lamb, that it is lawful to take an eye for an eye, that Jesus said, "I am the resurrection and the life."

Most of these verses, it is true, are chiefly remarkable for the vivid images they evoke, but certain stylistic effects are also created by their word patterns. When Melville's work is viewed as a whole, their recurrence takes on the nature of refrains. Each has the potential drama and the paradox he admired in all language, and some add linguistic appropriateness to the context into which they are introduced. When Melville said of Billy Budd that he had little "trace of the wisdom of the serpent, nor yet quite a dove,"[4]

---

[4] *Billy Budd and Other Prose Pieces*, p. 16.

he employed antithesis, which extended beyond his style to his theme. The Confidence-Man indulges in exaggeration, a significant habit of his, when he inquires if Polonius's advice to Laertes contains " 'Anything like "sell all thou hast and give to the poor?" ' "[5]

As might be expected, proverbs are prominent among those verses of Scripture which Melville repeatedly quoted, for he admired this form in both sacred and secular literature. But here it was easier for him to fall into trite or clerical tones. He asserted that the love of money is the root of evil, the bay-tree of the wicked will not flourish, the hairs of our head are numbered, pride goes before a fall, the wages of sin is death, the poor we have always with us, the wind bloweth where it listeth, there is a friend who sticketh closer than a brother.

Indeed, Melville was much better when imitating than when paraphrasing Biblical proverbs, and his quotation of them is most successful when his purpose is humorous. The remora or sucking-fish is described in *Mardi*: "Leech-like, it sticketh closer than a false brother in prosperity. . . ."[6] The amiably cynical Ishmael observes, apropos of receiving wages as a sailor: "The urbane activity with which a man receives money is really marvellous, considering that we so earnestly believe money to be the root of all earthly ills, and that on no account can a monied man enter heaven."[7]

Besides these actual proverbs, other Biblical idioms which have almost proverbial strength reappear on Melville's pages. Most of them occur in more than one verse, often in more than one book, and such common parlance have they become that they may be derived from many secondary sources as well. Among them are such adverbs and pronouns as *verily, whoso, forasmuch as;* such phrases

[5] *The Confidence-Man*, p. 228.
[6] *Mardi*, I, 62.
[7] *Moby-Dick*, I, 6.

as "vanity of vanities," "came to pass," "gathered to his fathers," "children's children," "fullness of time," "Ancient of Days," "peace of God," "Prince of Peace," "outer darkness," "the Rose of Sharon," "the fat of the land," "the quick and the dead," "weeping and wailing and gnashing of teeth," "the apple of his eye," "the salt of the earth."

These phrases and these proverbs, it is true, are among the most familiar verses in the Bible, and their occurrence in any voluminous author would not be surprising. But by no means all Melville's Scriptural echoes are so ordinary. The forecastle of the *Pequod,* where the off-duty watch is asleep, is said to resemble "some illuminated shrine of canonised kings and counsellors."[8] As the fog rises from the landscape in *Clarel* the Swede chants:

> "God came from Teman; in His hour
> The Holy One from Paran came. . . ."[9]

Lookout Mountain is pictured as the battle rages on it:

> Who inhabiteth the Mountain
>   That it shines in lurid light,
> And is rolled about with thunders,
>   And terrors, and a blight,
> Like Kaf the peak of Eblis—
>   Kaf, the evil height?
> Who has gone up with a shouting
>   And a trumpet in the night?[10]

Bomba's son exclaims amid his luxurious surroundings,

---

[8] *Ibid.,* II, 183. "For now should I have lain still and been quiet, I should have slept: then had I been at rest, With kings and counsellors of the earth. . ." (Job 3:13-14).

[9] *Clarel,* II, 7. "God came from Teman, and the Holy One from Mount Paran" (Hab. 3:3).

[10] *Poems,* p. 65. "For thus saith the high and lofty One that inhabiteth eternity, whose name is Holy; I dwell in the high and holy place. . ." (Isa. 57:15). "God is gone up with a shout, the Lord with the sound of a trumpet" (Ps. 47:5).

"Come, take thine ease; lean back, my soul...."[11] The ill-assorted crew of the *Pequod,* including as it does numerous islanders, is called an "Anacharsis Clootz deputation from all the isles of the sea."[12]

Without doubt the most interesting aspect of Melville's quotation from the Bible is his least faithful adherence to it; that is, his paraphrase of certain verses. As he inclined toward parallel rather than allegory in characterization and plot, so he preferred approximate to exact quotation. He employed different forms of the same words:

> "But Bel shall bow
> And Nebo stoop."[13]

Nehemiah, whose speech is more Scriptural than that of any other character of Melville's, says:

> "Lord, now Thou goest forth from Seir;
> Lord, now from Edom marchest Thou!"[14]

Two or more verses are often combined. Pierre inquires of Lucy: "Loveth she me with the love past all understanding?"[15] And Redburn, sympathizing with mistreated truck horses in Liverpool, declares: "Thou shalt not lay stripes upon these Roman citizens. . . ."[16] Occasionally an interpolation is made in the middle of a verse. Fat men are said to be of men "the good measures; brimmed, heaped, pressed down, piled up, and running over."[17]

Most effective of all, Melville followed the same structural pattern, retaining certain key words and substituting

---

[11] *Poems,* p. 386. "And I will say to my soul, Soul, thou hast much goods laid up for many years; take thine ease, eat, drink, and be merry" (Luke 12:19).

[12] *Moby-Dick,* I, 149. "Wherefore glorify ye the LORD in the fires, even the name of the LORD God of Israel in the isles of the sea" (Isa. 24:15).

[13] *Clarel,* I, 186. "Bel boweth down, Nebo stoopeth. . ." (Isa. 46:1).

[14] *Ibid.,* I, 219. "Lord, when thou wentest out of Seir, when Thou marchest out of the field of Edom. . ." (Judg. 5:4).

[15] *Pierre,* p. 125. John 21:15-17; Phil. 4:7.

[16] *Redburn,* p. 253. Exod. 20:1-17; Acts 22:25.

[17] *Mardi,* I, 337. Luke 6:38.

others in the subordinate positions. John Jermin, the mate of the *Julia,* had one failing: "he abhorred all weak infusions, and cleaved manfully to strong drink."[18] Among Oh-Oh's relics is a pouch made of an albatross's foot which was "Originally the property of a notorious old Tooth-per-Tooth."[19] Taji expresses his appreciation of Jarl because he did "with Samaritan charity bind up the rents, and pour needle and thread into the frightful gashes that agonised my hapless nether integuments, which thou calledst 'ducks. . . .'"[20] Continuing to repair their clothes as the pair sailed along in the little *Parki,* Jarl "laid down patch upon patch, and at long intervals precept upon precept; here several saws, and there innumerable stitches."[21] Ishmael holds a brief for animals slain by man for food:

I tell you it will be more tolerable for the Feegee that salted down a lean missionary in his cellar against a coming famine; it will be more tolerable for that provident Feegee, I say, in the day of judgment, than for thee, civilised and enlightened gourmand, who nailest geese to the ground and feastest on their bloated livers in thy paté-de-foie-gras.[22]

By no means all Melville's paraphrase, however, is so felicitous. These attempts are successful partly because the original meaning as well as the original phrasing is altered; in the new association which is made a new image is usually created. When, however, he offered no new association and merely rewrote the verse, the result is awkward, especially so when the original is itself a distinguished piece of prose or poetry. Thus, when he determined to adapt such passages as the Twenty-third Psalm he was at a double disadvantage. Nehemiah speaks:

[18] *Omoo,* p. 13; Rom. 12:9.
[19] *Mardi,* II, 70; Exod. 21:24, *et passim.*
[20] *Ibid.,* I, 17; Luke 10:34.
[21] *Ibid.,* I, 54; Isa. 28:10,13.
[22] *Moby-Dick,* II, 23; Matt. 10:15, *et passim.*

"Though through the valley of the shade
I pass, no evil do I fear;
His candle shineth on my head:
Lo, He is with me, even here."[23]

Vine laments at the sight of Jerusalem:

"How solitary on the hill
Sitteth the city; and how still—
How still!"[24]

The prophetic description of the Messiah is applied in *Clarel* to a leper:

"He lives forbid;
From him our faces have we hid;
No heart desires him, none redress,
He hath nor form nor comeliness;
For a transgressor he's suspected,
Behold, he is a thing infected,
Smitten of God, by men rejected."[25]

Now these quotations and paraphrases in Melville's prose and poetry are notable not alone for themselves but also for the influence they exert on the context in which they appear. That is, besides borrowing the exact words of a verse of Scripture, Melville often fell into Biblical idiom immediately preceding or following the actual excerpt. The style is contagious. From quotation he proceeded to imitation.

Sometimes the quoted portion is but the germ of an extended imitative passage. Such, for example, is Father Mapple's sermon, with its words from the book of Jonah scattered through the discourse and its conclusion in the style of the greater Hebrew prophets. Likewise the speech of Charles Noble in *The Confidence-Man*, having a few verses from Proverbs as its core, is the occasion for a long

---

[23] *Clarel*, I, 291.   [24] *Ibid.*, I, 136.
[25] *Ibid.*, I, 101-102.

discourse in the manner of that book and of Psalms. Briefer instances of this influence may be cited in great number.
Redburn's description of the American melting pot is one:

The other world beyond this, which was longed for by the
devout before Columbus' time, was found in the New; and the
deep-sea land, that first struck these soundings, brought up the
soil of Earth's Paradise. Not a Paradise then, or now; but to
be made so at God's good pleasure, and in the fulness and mellowness of time. The seed is sown, and the harvest must come;
and our children's children, on the world's jubilee morning,
shall all go with their sickles to the reaping. Then shall the
curse of Babel be revoked, a new Pentecost come, and the language they shall speak shall be the language of Britain. French-
men, and Danes, and Scots; and the dwellers on the shores of
the Mediterranean, and in the regions round about; Italians,
and Indians, and Moors; there shall appear unto them cloven
tongues as of fire.[26]

This passage actually contains but one quotation from
a particular verse in the Bible: ". . . there shall appear unto
them cloven tongues as of fire."[27] The Biblical echoes, however, of vocabulary, of syntax, of idiom, are numerous.
"God's good pleasure" is a Germanism, borrowed appropriately from the Lukan promise that the kingdom will be
given to the chosen people. "Fulness and mellowness of
time" exemplifies the genitive of attribute—as well as being
a paraphrase of a familiar Biblical idiom, "children's children" and "the language they shall speak shall be the language of Britain" are cognate constructions, and "regions
round about" is a use of compound prepositions, all of which
are common in Hebrew. The reference to a jubilee calls to
mind the ancient Jewish celebration, at which time, however, there was to be no sowing or reaping; Melville's
image of the harvest is thus misplaced here. The inverted

[26] *Redburn*, p. 217.
[27] "And there appeared unto them cloven tongues like as of fire, and it
sat upon each of them" (Acts 2:3).

order of the clause, "Then shall the curse of Babel be revoked," is reminiscent of the speeches of the King in
Matthew's account of the Last Judgment: "Then shall the
King say unto them on his right hand. . . ." "Dwellers
on the shores of the Mediterranean" comes apparently from
the ninth verse of the same chapter of Acts from which
the actual quotation in the passage is about to be made:
"Parthians, and Medes, and Elamites, and the dwellers in
Mesopotamia, and in Judaea, and Cappadocia, in Pontus,
and Asia. . . ."

So Melville surrounded other Biblical allusions with
Biblical forms not properly part of the allusions themselves.
In assigning this quotation to its Old Testament author he
dropped into an archaism, presumably scriptural to his
mind: " 'Thou art as a lion of the waters, and as a dragon
of the sea,' saith Ezekiel. . . ."[28] The same verb form occurs
in Ishmael's reference to "the Holy One that sitteth there
white like wool."[29] Again, he employed "how" with the
pronoun "that" when paraphrasing Paul, a construction appearing in certain books of the New Testament—Corinthians, James, Jude: "Bethink thee of that saying of St.
Paul in Corinthians, about corruption and incorruption;
how that we are sown in dishonour, but raised in glory."[30]
The use of "even" as an intensive, another archaism common in Scripture, is inserted in Melville's quotation from
the Psalmist as he wonders in "Cockle-doodle-doo" "whether, indeed, the glorious cock would prove game even from
the rising of the sun unto the going down thereof."[31]

II

From such paraphrases as these, superficial echoes
though they seem, it is but a step to Melville's actual imitation of his source and his transformation of both its style

[28] *Moby-Dick*, II, 102.   [29] *Ibid.*, I, 235.
[30] *Ibid.*, II, 162.   [31] *Billy Budd and Other Prose Pieces*, p. 153.

and his own. Not so great a variety of Biblical strains inspired him thus deeply, but the three which did are notable ones themselves: those of prophecy, of the Psalms, and of the apocalypses. The first two are the most distinguished styles to be found in all the Bible, in which subjects also dear to Melville's heart were discussed. All are styles with tremendous dramatic and lyric possibilities.

The prophetic strain is present in *Moby-Dick*, where among numerous characters who may be compared with the Jewish prophets one actually speaks their language: Father Mapple. The first part of his sermon incorporates a dozen quotations from the book of Jonah and many Biblical idioms: "cast him forth," "spake unto the fish," "the word of the Lord." But in the last two paragraphs he himself falls into the rhythm of the Old Testament. He adopts a familiar linguistic device of the Hebrew prophets—of Jeremiah, Isaiah, and Ezekiel in particular—the interjection "woe" repeatedly introducing a sentence:

"Woe to him whom this world charms from Gospel duty! Woe to him who seeks to pour oil upon the waters when God has brewed them into a gale! Woe to him who seeks to please rather than to appal! Woe to him whose good name is more to him than goodness! Woe to him who, in this world, courts not dishonour! Woe to him who would not be true, even though to be false were salvation! Yea, woe to him who, as the great Pilot Paul has it, while preaching to others is himself a castaway!"[32]

The number of "woes" which occur in this passage is itself worthy of note. There are seven, a number often occurring in the structures of Biblical literature. The form of Jeremiah's Babylonian prophecy is a sevenfold denunciation, the central section of which is a sevenfold image of doom.[33] Whether or not Melville was aware of this divi-

[32] *Moby-Dick*, I, 58-59.
[33] Jer. 50, 51. The sections are: judgment on Bel (50:1-5); God's people as sheep devoured (50:6-20); the idea of recompense (50:21-32); the seven-

sion, which is not apparent in the arrangement of verses in the King James Version, must, of course, remain doubtful. But the similarity of form is of particular interest in view of his reading of Jeremiah and of the apparent echoes of the prophet's thought in Father Mapple's discourse.

Also typical of Hebrew prophecy is the element of contrast in Mapple's conclusion. The balance of each sentence in his denunciation, and even its paradox, echoes such words as these of Isaiah's, marked in Melville's Bible: "Woe unto them that call evil good, and good evil; that put darkness for light, and light for darkness; that put bitter for sweet, and sweet for bitter!"[34] The more general contrast between the warning of the first and the consolation of the next paragraph is best matched by Joel, with his opening vision of the locust plague and his concluding scene in the holy mountain. But the twenty-fifth chapter of Jeremiah, foretelling the Captivity, and the thirtieth, promising the Return, form a similar contrast. Both chapters in Melville's Bible have many markings.

Yet while the thought is antithetical, the structure of these two paragraphs in *Moby-Dick* is parallel: the seven "woes" are followed by six "delights." The liturgical form thus achieved is most comparable to Luke's use of four "woes" to succeed his four beatitudes, a passage which Melville marked in his Testament.

More than the structure of prophecy, however, informs Father Mapple's "delights"; its phraseology also is echoed:

"Delight is to him, who gives no quarter in the truth, and kills, burns, and destroys all sin though he pluck it out from

---

fold image of the sword, drought, destroying wind, cankerworm, battle-axe, destroying mountain, threshing floor (50:33-51:40); judgment on Bel (51:41-44); people of Israel delivered (51:45-53); idea of recompense (51:54-64) (Richard G. Moulton, *The Modern Reader's Bible*, New York, 1907, pp. 600-607).

[34] Isa. 5:20.

under the robes of Senators and Judges. Delight,—top-gallant delight is to him, who acknowledges no law or lord, but the Lord his God, and is only a patriot to heaven. Delight is to him, whom all the waves of the billows of the seas of the boisterous mob can never shake from this sure Keel of the Ages. And eternal delight and deliciousness will be his, who coming to lay him down, can say with his final breath—O Father!—chiefly known to me by Thy rod—mortal or immortal, here I die. I have striven to be Thine, more than to be this world's, or mine own. Yet this is nothing; I leave eternity to Thee; for what is man that he should live out the lifetime of his God?"[35]

The opening sentence of this passage recalls, though there is but one word common to both, the message of Jehovah to Jeremiah, commanding him also to search out sin in high places: "See, I have this day set thee over the nations and over the kingdoms, to root out, and to pull down, and to destroy, and to throw down, to build, and to plant."[36] In the sentence following are phrases from the books of several prophets. The use of "acknowledge" occurs in Daniel and Isaiah, as well as in Proverbs ("In all thy ways acknowledge him"), and in I John. "No law or lord" is reminiscent of "the law of the Lord," appearing not only in such prophecies as those of Isaiah, Jeremiah, and Amos, but in other books of the Old and in the New Testament. Its most memorable use is probably in the First Psalm: "But his delight is in the law of the Lord." As for the double appellation, "the Lord his God," it is, with variations of the personal pronoun, to be found in almost every book of the Bible. When Father Mapple speaks next of "all the waves of the billows of the seas"—a succession of genitives which is a Hebraism—he is echoing Jonah's prayer: "For thou hadst cast me into the deep, in the midst of the seas; and the floods compassed me about: all thy billows and thy waves passed over me."[37] And when he avers that they "can

[35] *Moby-Dick*, I, 59.   [36] Jer. 1:10.
[37] Jonah 2:3.

never shake" him, he suggests the words of another prophet, Haggai:

Yet once, it is a little while, and I will shake the heavens, and the earth, and the sea, and the dry land;
   And I will shake all nations. . . .[38]

The use of "rod" in the sense in which Father Mapple employs it, "O Father! chiefly known to me by Thy rod," is familiar in Job, Psalms, Proverbs, Isaiah, Lamentations. Melville marked the verse in Isaiah beginning, "O Assyrian, the rod of mine anger."[39] And as the Psalmist cried, in a verse he also noted, "What is man, that thou art mindful of him?"[40] the whalemen's preacher queried, "for what is man that he should live out the lifetime of his God?" The cognate accusative, "live out the lifetime," is another Hebraism, and "to lay him down" is an archaic use of the reflexive form of this verb common in the Bible.

In connection with this interest of Melville's in the prophetic style of the Bible it may be remarked that the use of the catalogue was one of its general characteristics. For, although this device does not appear in Mapple's sermon, it was, of course, a favorite of Melville's. A notable example from the Old Testament is Jeremiah's catalogue of kings, which is not unlike Melville's lists of ships, temples, and sailors:

Then took I the cup at the LORD's hand, and made all the nations to drink, unto whom the LORD had sent me:
   To wit, Jerusalem, and the cities of Judah, and the kings thereof, and the princes thereof, to make them a desolation, an astonishment, an hissing, and a curse; as it is this day;
   Pharaoh king of Egypt, and his servants, and his princes, and all his people;
   And all the mingled people, and all the kings of the land of Uz, and all the kings of the land of the Philistines, and Ash-

[38] Hag. 2:6-7. See also Heb. 12:26-27.
[39] Isa. 10:5.   [40] Ps. 8:4. See also Job 7:17.

kelon, and Azzah, and Ekron, and the remnant of Ashdod,
Edom, and Moab, and the children of Ammon,
And all the kings of Tyrus, and all the kings of Zidon, and
the kings of the isles which are beyond the sea,
Dedan, and Tema, and Buz, and all that are in the utmost
corners,
And all the kings of Arabia, and all the kings of the mingled
people that dwell in the desert,
And all the kings of Zimri, and all the kings of Elam, and
all the kings of the Medes,
And all the kings of the north, far and near, one with another, and all the kingdoms of the world, which are upon the
face of the earth: and the king of Sheshach shall drink after
them.[41]

The style of Psalms is imitated in *Pierre* and *The Confidence-Man*, as the prophets are in *Moby-Dick*. As Pierre
and Lucy ride into the country in the morning the author
breaks into a prose paean which has many of the characteristics of a Hebrew poem:

Oh, praised be the beauty of this earth; the beauty, and the
bloom, and the mirthfulness thereof! The first worlds made
were winter worlds; the second made, were vernal worlds; the
third, and last, and perfectest, was this summer world of ours.
In the cold and nether spheres preachers preach of earth, as we of
Paradise above. Oh, there, my friends, they say, they have a
season, in their language known as summer. Then their fields
spin themselves green carpets; snow and ice are not in all the
land; then a million strange, bright, fragrant things powder that
sward with perfumes; and high, majestic beings, dumb and
grand, stand up with outstretched arms, and hold their green
canopies over merry angels—men and women—who love and
wed, and sleep and dream, beneath the approving glances of
their visible god and goddess, glad-hearted sun, and pensive
moon!
Oh, praised be the beauty of this earth; the beauty, and the
bloom, and the mirthfulness thereof. We lived before, and shall

[41] Jer. 25:17-26. The verses immediately following are marked in Melville's
Bible.

live again; and as we hope for a fairer world than this to come; so we came from one less fine. From each successive world, the demon Principle is more and more dislodged; he is the accursed clog from chaos, and thither, by every new translation, we drive him further and further back again. Hosannahs to this world! so beautiful itself, and the vestibule to more. Out of some past Egypt, we have come to this new Canaan, and from this new Canaan, we press on to some Circassia. Though still the villains, Want and Woe, followed us out of Egypt, and now beg in Canaan's streets: yet Circassia's gates shall not admit them; they, with their sire, the demon Principle, must back to chaos, whence they came.[42]

It is the form rather than the subject of this passage which imitates the Bible, for the Hebrew poets rarely noticed nature except pantheistically, or addressed praise directly to an abstraction, as Melville did here. However, its vocabulary and its rhythm unmistakably echo the Psalms. The words "praised be," "thereof," "Hosannahs," and "out of Egypt" are all employed by the Psalmist. His general principle of form, too, is followed. There is a refrain introducing each paragraph; there is alternation between the exclamation of exultation and the detailing of matter on which the exultation is founded; there is, in the first half of each paragraph, a stanzaic pattern, consisting of a distich and a tristich in the first, a distich and a tetrastich in the second. If the passages are printed as poetry this pattern is clearly revealed:

> Oh, praised be the beauty of this earth;
> the beauty, and the bloom, and the mirthfulness thereof!
>
> The first worlds made were winter worlds;
> the second made, were vernal worlds;
> the third, and last, and perfectest, was this summer world
> of ours. . . .

[42] *Pierre*, pp. 43-44.

Oh, praised be the beauty of this earth;
the beauty, and the bloom, and the mirthfulness thereof.

We lived before,
and shall live again;
and as we hope for a fairer world than this to come;
so we came from one less fine.

Now the fundamental characteristic of all Semitic poetry, not known to the translators of the King James Version
but fully discovered by Melville's day, is parallelism. The
balance is one of thought rather than of syllable, and it is in
general a simple balance. The two-line parallel or distich
is the norm, with variations of the tristich and the tetrastich. Of numerous possible examples in Psalms the following lines, arranged to reveal the extent of their parallelism, may be placed beside Melville's "psalm" for comparison:

Sing unto the Lord with thanksgiving;
Sing praise upon the harp unto our God:

Who covereth the heaven with clouds,
who prepareth rain for the earth,
who maketh grass to grow upon the mountains. . . .

He giveth snow like wool:
he scattereth the hoarfrost like ashes.

He casteth forth his ice like morsels:
who can stand before his cold?

He sendeth out his word,
and melteth them:
he causeth his wind to blow,
and the waters flow.[43]

Another imitation of Psalms appears in *The Confidence-
Man*. The spokesman is Charles Noble, who thus celebrates
the wine press:

[43] Ps. 147:7-8, 16-18.

" 'Praise be unto the press, not Faust's, but Noah's; let us extol and magnify the press, the true press of Noah, from which breaketh the true morning. Praise be unto the press, not the black press but the red; let us extol and magnify the press, the red press of Noah, from which cometh inspiration. Ye pressman of the Rhineland and the Rhine, join in with all ye who tread out the glad tidings on isle Madeira or Mitylene.—Who giveth redness of eyes by making men long to tarry at the fine print?—Praise be unto the press, the rosy press of Noah, which giveth rosiness of hearts, by making men long to tarry at the rosy wine.—Who hath babblings and contentions? Who, without cause, inflicteth wounds? Praise be unto the press, the kindly press of Noah, which knitteth friends, which fuseth foes.— Who may be bribed?—Who may be bound?—Praise be unto the press, the free press of Noah, which will not lie for tyrants, but make tyrants speak the truth.—Then praise be unto the press, the frank old press of Noah; then let us extol and magnify the press, the brave old press of Noah; then let us with roses garland and enwreath the press, the grand old press of Noah, from which flow streams of knowledge which give man a bliss no more unreal than his pain.' "[44]

Actually the central part of this paragraph is a paraphrase of three verses from Proverbs:

Who hath woe? who hath sorrow? who hath contentions? who hath babbling? who hath wounds without cause? who hath redness of eyes?

They that tarry long at the wine; they that go to seek mixed wine.

Look not thou upon the wine when it is red, when it giveth his colour in the cup, when it moveth itself aright.[45]

In addition to his adaptation of these words, Melville caught the Biblical tone by the use of the Psalmist's "extol," "magnify," and "praise be unto"; by the archaic "giveth," "knitteth," "fuseth," "ye." "Breaketh the true morning" suggests

[44] *The Confidence-Man*, p. 223.
[45] Prov. 23:29-31.

Isaiah ("Then shall thy light break forth as the morning")[46] and "glad tidings" is from Luke and Paul. The allusion to Noah, of course, is to the account of his drunkenness.

In Noble's speech again, as in *Pierre,* there seems to be an imitation of the form of Hebrew poetry. This passage is even more antiphonal, as may be seen if its refrains are separated from the rest of the paragraph. It will then read as though its parts have been assigned to different speakers or choruses:

First chorus:

Praise be unto the press, not Faust's, but Noah's;
let us extol and magnify the press, the true press of Noah,
from which breaketh the true morning.

Praise be unto the press, not the black press, but the red;
let us extol and magnify the press, the red press of Noah,
from which cometh inspiration.

Second chorus:

Ye pressman of the Rhineland and the Rhine, join
in with all ye who tread out the glad tidings
on isle Madeira or Mitylene.

Who giveth redness of eyes by making men long to tarry
at the fine print?

First chorus:

Praise be unto the press, the rosy press of Noah,
which giveth rosiness of hearts,
by making men long to tarry at the rosy wine.

Second chorus:

Who hath babblings and contentions?
Who, without cause, inflicteth wounds?

First chorus:

Praise be unto the press, the kindly press of Noah,
which knitteth friends, which fuseth foes.

[46] Isa. 58:8.

Second chorus:

Who may be bribed?
Who may be bound?

First chorus:

Praise be unto the press, the free press of Noah,
which will not lie for tyrants, but make tyrants
    speak the truth.

Full chorus:

Then praise be unto the press, the frank old press of Noah;
then let us extol and magnify the press, the brave old press
    of Noah;
then let us with roses garland and enwreath the press, the
    grand old press of Noah,
from which flow streams of knowledge
which give man a bliss no more unreal than his pain.

The Psalms which are most antiphonal and seem to be
written, like Noble's poem, for more than one speaker or
singer are the so-called Hallel Psalms. The 149th and 150th
are examples; these may be divided thus for actual recital:

First chorus:

Sing unto the LORD a new song,
And his praise in the assembly of the saints.
Let Israel rejoice in him that made him:
Let the children of Zion be joyful in their King.
Let them praise his name in the dance:
Let them sing praises unto him with the timbrel and harp.

Second chorus:

For the LORD taketh pleasure in his people:
He will beautify the meek with salvation.

First chorus:

Let the saints exult in glory:
Let them sing for joy upon their beds.
Let the high praises of God be in their mouth,
And a two-edged sword in their hand:

Second chorus:

To execute vengeance upon the nations,
And punishments upon the peoples;
To bind their kings with chains,
And their nobles with fetters of iron;
To execute upon them the judgement written:
This honour have all his saints.

First chorus:

Praise God in his sanctuary:

Second chorus:

Praise him in the firmament of his power.

First chorus:

Praise him for his mighty acts:

Second chorus:

Praise him according to his excellent greatness.

First chorus:

Praise him with the sound of the trumpet:

Second chorus:

Praise him with the psaltery and harp.

First chorus:

Praise him with the timbrel and dance:

Second chorus:

Praise him with stringed instruments and the pipe.

First chorus:

Praise him upon the loud cymbals:

Second chorus:

Praise him upon the high sounding cymbals.

Full chorus:

Let every thing that hath breath praise the LORD.[47]

[47] Moulton, *op. cit.*, pp. 874-875.

The style in which the apocalypses of the Bible are written is also echoed by Melville, though, it is true, this style is less easily distinguished than that of the prophets and the Psalmist. The seers had fewer linguistic peculiarities, and their single interest was to describe what they had seen. Yet as they saw something beyond sight, they described it in language which differed from that of their narration and exposition.

So when, in *Mardi, Moby-Dick, Pierre, Clarel,* and *Billy Budd,* Melville related visions which have counterparts in the Bible, he not only borrowed certain images but fell into a style unlike that in which the rest of his narratives were told. In so doing he distinguished very little between apocalypses and drew upon them all in a manner which suggests the composite nature of the apocalyptic beasts themselves, with their unrelated limbs and features. For that matter, the seers did the same, combining elements from all who preceded them. So John echoed Isaiah, Ezekiel, and Daniel, to a lesser extent, Zechariah and Joel, yet achieved an effect all his own.

In *Mardi* Babbalanja's vision is reminiscent of several in Hebraic literature. An entire chapter is given to his story of the dream which came to him as he rested, "after I had laid me down," as he says, copying the Scriptural use of this verb as a reflexive. At first hearing a melody, he next sees a bright object:

"Thwarting the sky, it grew, and grew, descending; till bright wings were visible: between them, a pensive face angelic, downward beaming; and, for one golden moment, gauze-veiled in spangled Berenice's Locks.

"Then, as white flame from yellow, out from that starry cluster it emerged; and brushed the astral crosses, crowns, and cups. And as in violet, tropic seas, ships leave a radiant-white and fire-fly wake; so, in long extension tapering, behind the vision, gleamed another Milky Way.

"Strange throbbings seized me; my soul tossed on its own tides. But soon the inward harmony bounded in exulting choral strains. I heard a feathery rush; and straight beheld a form, traced all over with veins of vivid light. The vision undulated round me.

" 'Oh! spirit! angel! god! whate'er thou art,' I cried, 'leave me; I am but man.' "[48]

Now the central object of Babbalanja's vision has the traditional appearance of a heavenly being, and only its most general features suggest the winged creatures, usually suffused in fire, glimpsed by the apocalyptic writers of the Bible. His response to it, however, is, like theirs, notably like the celebrated lamentation of Isaiah before the seraphim: "Woe is me! for I am undone; because I am a man of unclean lips, and I dwell in the midst of a people of unclean lips: for mine eyes have seen the King, the LORD of hosts."[49]

The prospect which Babbalanja views with this heavenly creature is "a new heaven,"[50] a phrase suggestive of the scene which met the eye of John as he was also conducted by an angel: "And I saw a new heaven and a new earth. . . ."[51] Yet this is only the first stage in Babbalanja's celestial tour. As they talk, he and his guide are joined by an angel of a higher order, who is hailed as an archangel by the first spirit, in his turn echoing Babbalanja's words of humility.

For the purpose of Babbalanja's spiritual journey is to lead him not immediately but by degrees into the divine presence. This progression and part of his conversation with the archangel recall the experience of Esdras, who learned of ever greater mysteries with each seven-day period of fasting, and who, like Babbalanja, received little satisfaction in answer to his query about the reason for evil. In *Mardi*, however, the arrangement of creation into sep-

---

[48] *Mardi*, II, 373-374.
[50] *Mardi*, II, 374.
[49] Isa. 6:5.
[51] Rev. 21:1.

arate spheres is neo-Platonic, and the landscape is Miltonic
or Dantesque, as the archangel transports them to a higher
heaven, also flaming, and inhabited by spirits resembling
"broad-winged crimson-dyed flamingos."[52] The first angel's
assertion, too, that all heaven is formed of love suggests the
Paradiso. But the image at the culmination of Babbalanja's
vision is again Hebraic:

"As poised, we hung in this rapt ether, a sudden trembling
seized the four wings now folding me. And afar off, in zones
still upward reaching, suns' orbits off, I, tranced, beheld an
awful glory. Sphere in sphere, it burned:—the one Shekinah!
The air was flaked with fire;—deep in which fell showers of
silvery globes, tears magnified—braiding the flame with rain-
bows. I heard a sound; but not for me, nor my first guide,
was that unutterable utterance. Then, my second guide was
swept aloft, as rises a cloud of red-dyed leaves in autumn
whirlwinds."[53]

The conception of the Shekinah was, in fact, later in Jewish thought than the Old Testament canon. It does not occur in Scripture at all but in the Aramaic Targums, whose
expositors, reluctant to describe God in terms suggestive of
anthropomorphism, made substitutes for his name in those
passages which in any fashion localized him. Among the
substitutes were the Word, the Spirit, the Shekinah, the
latter signifying the earthly dwelling of the Deity. It must
have been a conception attractive to Melville, with his tendency to dehumanize the nature of truth, to push it beyond the bounds of speech or attainment. He referred to it
again, and again associated it with an image of fire: the
phosphorescent ocean in *Clarel,* to which the sky at Jesus's
birth is compared, is called a Shekinah. The use of the
word on each occasion defines rather significantly the vision
which he is describing: it is not the ultimate reality itself

[52] *Mardi*, II, 377.
[53] *Ibid.*, II, 378.

which is revealed but only a manifestation of it. In his most dramatic apocalypses, Melville never, like John, saw the Lamb on his throne. The emanating brightness was as close as he came.

In *Moby-Dick* the apocalypses of the Bible are brought most fully to mind by Gabriel, with his name taken from Daniel and his property, the seventh vial, from Revelation. But his rhythms are not those of the Jewish seers:

"Think, think of the fevers, yellow and bilious! Beware of the horrible plague!

. . . .

"Think, think of thy whale-boat, stoven and sunk! Beware of the horrible tail!"[54]

Ishmael himself comes nearer to them. In the chapter entitled "The Whiteness of the Whale" he cites the twenty-four elders who are clad in white and who stand before the great white throne on which sits the Lamb, as white as wool. In this same vein he describes his feelings upon seeing his first albatross:

At intervals, it arched forth its vast archangel wings, as if to embrace some holy ark. Wondrous flutterings and throbbings shook it. Though bodily unharmed, it uttered cries, as some king's ghost in supernatural distress. Through its inexpressible, strange eyes, methought I peeped to secrets which took hold of God. As Abraham before the angels, I bowed myself; the white thing was so white, its wings so wide, and in those forever exiled waters, I had lost the miserable warping memories of traditions and of towns. Long I gazed at that prodigy of plumage. I cannot tell, can only hint, the things that darted through me then.[55]

The bird had been caught by a hook and line, and after fastening on it a leathern tally inscribed with the ship's position, the captain released it. Ishmael continues: "But

[54] *Moby-Dick*, II, 42. [55] *Ibid.*, I, 236-237.

I doubt not, that leathern tally, meant for man, was taken off in Heaven, when the white fowl flew to join the wing-folding, the invoking, and adoring cherubim!"[56]

The albatross is thus associated with two accounts of the cherubim. "Some holy ark" refers to the ark of the covenant, described in Kings, whereon golden figures of them were fixed, their wings outspread to support the mercy seat. But the "wing-folding, the invoking, and adoring cherubim" seems to be from Revelation, where the throne of God is surrounded by four winged beasts which praise him ceaselessly. For though they are not called cherubim there, it is generally assumed that they are, since their forms are similar to Ezekiel's cherubim.

All heavenly beings were, in fact, alike to Melville—cherubim and seraphim, angels and archangels. He distinguished only between good and evil supernatural creatures, not between the hierarchies of each group. Glibly Ishmael wrote of the spectacle of the peaking of the whale's flukes: "But in gazing at such scenes, it is all in what mood you are in; if in the Dantean, the devils will occur to you; if in that of Isaiah, the archangels."[57] Yet neither Isaiah nor any other Old Testament seer has anything to say of archangels. They are a feature of the Hebrew celestial hierarchy which first appeared in the Apocrypha.

Pierre, too, who exclaims, " 'I will gospelise the world anew, and show them deeper secrets than the Apocalypse!' "[58] combines more than one Biblical vision in his own. When he receives the note from Lucy, he holds "the artless, angelical letter in his unrealising hand," and asks "whether this was the place that an angel should choose for its visit to earth." He feels that he has received a kind of revelation:

[56] *Ibid.,* I, 237.
[57] *Ibid.,* II, 122.
[58] *Pierre,* p. 381.

When surrounded by the base and mercenary crew, man, too long wonted to eye his race with a suspicious disdain, suddenly is brushed by some angelical plume of humanity, and the human accents of superhuman love, and the human eyes of superhuman beauty and glory, suddenly burst on his being; then how wonderful and fearful the shock! It is as if the sky-cope were rent, and from the black valley of Jehoshaphat, he caught upper glimpses of the seraphim in the visible act of adoring.[59]

Here Melville has transported the six-winged seraphim, mentioned only by Isaiah, from their place above Jehovah's throne to the valley between Jerusalem and the Mount of Olives, generally identified as the scene of the Last Judgment. Thus Joel pictured it, making it appear a "black valley" by his prediction that the sun and moon should on that occasion be darkened.

In *Clarel* and in *Billy Budd* the two visions combined are from the New Testament: the Ascension of Jesus and the Lamb on the throne. The image linking the two is the comparison of the clouds, into which Jesus disappeared, to the fleece of the Lamb. In *Clarel* the palmer Arculf describes to his friends on the isle of Iona the appearance of the Palestinian sky on Ascension Eve:

> "Olivet gleams then much the same—
> Caressed, curled over, yea, encurled
> By fleecy fires which typic be:
> O Lamb of God! O Light o' the World!"[60]

The figure is repeated in *Billy Budd,* when the eastern sky on the morning of Billy's execution is said to resemble "the fleece of the Lamb of God" and when it is concluded that into this sky "Billy ascended."[61]

Now if it is true that there are fewer distinctive features in the apocalyptic style than in those of the prophets and

[59] *Ibid.*, p. 433. [60] *Clarel*, I, 141-142.
[61] *Billy Budd and Other Prose Pieces*, p. 103.

the Psalmist, it may nevertheless be said that there is one stylistic feature necessary to all vision literature. In this literature the effectiveness of the words depends upon their sound as much as upon their meaning. The scene described is not of this world, and to be transported into it the reader must be stirred emotionally. Hence, the music of such visions as Revelation is as important as the machinery of their imagery.

The music of this book, in fact, is typical of much that is in other books of its kind. Its most impressive passages, in the Greek as well as the King James translation, are dominated by the same general sounds: long, open vowels and liquid, singing consonants. At the same time there is a more rolling rhythm, a longer length of line than is usual in straight Biblical narrative. The adoration of the cherubim is an example:

And the four beasts had each of them six wings about him; and they were full of eyes within: and they rest not day and night, saying, Holy, holy, holy, Lord God Almighty, which was, and is, and is to come.

And when those beasts give glory and honour and thanks to him that sat on the throne, who liveth for ever and ever,

The four and twenty elders fall down before him that sat on the throne, and worship him that liveth for ever and ever, and cast their crowns before the throne, saying,

Thou art worthy, O Lord, to receive glory and honour and power: for thou hast created all things, and for thy pleasure they are and were created.[62]

It is interesting to find these same characteristics in Melville's imitation of Biblical apocalypses. The average length of his lines on these occasions is not longer. But in some passages, Ishmael's description of the albatross for example, the lines, which are short at the beginning, become longer in the middle of the paragraph, as at a climax,

[62] Rev. 4:8-11.

to be shortened again at the end. The movement seems to represent the approach to and retreat from a mount of revelation.

In these same passages, from *Mardi, Moby-Dick, Pierre, Clarel*, and *Billy Budd*, there is a preponderance of vowels which are sounded deep in the throat. The broad *a* is present in such words as *thwarting, starry, arch, ark, archangel, darted, unharmed, warping*. Other long vowels are heard in *radiant, flaked, embrace, vapoury, wake, tapering, Abraham, angels, strains, straight; white, wide, exiled, light, bright, fire, eyes, sky, tides; golden, adoring, folding, invoking, cope, holy, glory, moment, aloft, hold, rose, accord; secrets, gleamed, peeped, reaching, sweet, serene, fleece.*

The consonants include a large number of sibilants; *inexpressible, astral, brush, strange, descending, ascending, cluster, vision, tossed, distress, disdain, visible, ministering, mystical*. There are also a good many liquid consonants: *l's* in *flame, yellow, milky, globes, leathern, tally, flew, fowl, glimpses, plumage, undulated, flutterings; r's* in *grew, Berenice's, emerged, throbbings, harmony, rush, unutterable, burned, miserable, wondrous.*

These are rhythms and sounds, of course, which are intrinsically capable of arousing excitement and awe whatever their content, and Melville might have discovered the fact in any context. In Disraeli's *Curiosities of Literature*,[63] for example, he noted the observation that in the case of proper names, "the softness of delicious vowels, or the ruggedness of inexorable consonants" may actually have an effect on a man's happiness and fortune. In any case, whether or not he learned this lesson from the Hebrew seers and their translators, like them, Melville repeatedly dropped the flat tones and conversational rhythms of his narrative to become more sonorous and more rolling in the lightning flashes of his visions.

[63] Melville's copy is in the New York Public Library.

III

In addition to incorporating these quotations and these imitations of particular Biblical styles in his own, Melville occasionally fell into certain patterns of language characteristic of Hebrew literature in general. These turns of expression are present in all books of the Bible, though particularly of the Old Testament, and their occurrence in Melville does not constitute an allusion to a specific book or verse. From them, in fact, all Biblical content is absent. Thus they offer proof not only of the sensitivity of his ear but of his ability thoroughly to assimilate another style.

Melville's prose contains, first of all, numerous Hebraisms,[64] of which there are two varieties. Lexicographical Hebraisms, a literal rendering into English of a Hebrew word or combination of words which gives to English equivalents a usage and a connotation they do not have, may be exemplified by the word *seed,* used in the Bible to mean race or life. Melville used it thus more than once. But he incorporated more syntactical Hebraisms, that is, constructions due to a traditional English way of translating certain Hebrew idioms. The fact suggests again the extent to which the sound of Biblical language stirred him, influencing him to introduce in his pages such syntactical Hebraisms as a succession of genitives, the cognate accusative, superfluous prepositions, the combination of a noun and an auxiliary to form a verb, the use of the conjunction *for* to begin a sentence.

Aside from these Hebraisms, there are other characteristics of Hebrew literature which Melville seems to have recognized and copied: parallelism and antiphonalism, figures and proverbs. It was Bishop Lowth who first discovered parallelism to be the principle underlying all Hebrew poetry, a device prominent also in Hebrew prose.

---

[64] See William Rosenau, *Hebraisms in the Authorized Version of the Bible* (Baltimore, 1903).

According to his analysis, published in 1753 in *De sacra poesi Hebraeorum praelectiones academicae,* there are three kinds of parallelism: synonymous, antithetical, and synthetic. Not one but several examples may be found in Melville of each of these types: of the first, " 'Art thou more truly royal, than they were kings? Or more a man, that [*sic*] they were men?' ";[65] of the second, " 'And though want of suspicion more than want of sense, sometimes leads a man into harm, yet too much suspicion is as bad as too little sense' ";[66] of the third, " 'Happy we to groan, that our children's children may be glad.' "[67]

Akin to this parallelism is the antiphonalism of Hebrew literature. In the poetry, of course, it is an integral part of the form. But it is present also in the prose, sometimes the inevitable method of presenting the subject. In the process of representing Jehovah and the Israelites conversing with each other through the mediation of priests and prophets the authors of the Old Testament had to speak for more than one side. Hence they often employed question and answer: "Who shall ascend into the hill of the LORD? or who shall stand in his holy place? He that hath clean hands, and a pure heart. . . ."[68] So Babbalanja quotes from Bardianna: " ' "Who in Arcturus hath heard of us? They know us not in the Milky Way." ' "[69] A similar effect of versicle and response was achieved by the Hebrew lawgivers, succeeding generalization by example. Cried Isaiah:

Woe unto them that draw iniquity with cords of vanity, and sin as it were with a cart rope:

That say, Let him make speed, and hasten his work, that we may see it: and let the counsel of the Holy One of Israel draw nigh and come, that we may know it![70]

The same sequence is apparent throughout the chapter on "The Whiteness of the Whale" in *Moby-Dick,* as Ishmael follows his theories with illustrations:

[65] *Mardi,* I, 275. [66] *Israel Potter,* p. 52. [67] *Mardi,* I, 224.
[68] Ps. 24:3-4. [69] *Mardi,* II, 299. [70] Isa. 5:18-19.

Nor, in quite other aspects, does Nature in her least palpable but not the less malicious agencies, fail to enlist among her forces this crowning attribute of the terrible. From its snowy aspect, the gauntleted ghost of the Southern Seas has been denominated the White Squall.[71]

In such parallelism and such antiphonalism it is obvious that few connectives are needed. And in fact, the Hebrews had almost none to use. Since the conjunction *waw*, translated in the King James Version *and, but,* and *so,* was their only means of joining facts and ideas, their syntax was necessarily simple, consisting for the most part of co-ordinate clauses. Their language was thus incapable of expressing the most subtle modulations of thought, and in effect blocked their way to true reasoning. Within the Bible itself there is between the style of Samuel and that of Acts, which exhibits the influence of Greek rhetoric, the greatest difference.

Now a general looseness of connection is characteristic of all Melville's structure, making it particularly easy for him to employ such devices as catalogue and allusion, parallel and refrain, proverb and allegory. True, there is great variety in the length of his clauses, less important facts are subordinated, and his sequence is often strikingly inverted. But the tortuous writing in *Pierre* and *The Confidence-Man* is an attempt to represent feeling rather than thought. Compared with a contemporary like Henry James, Melville made few innovations in the order of his sentences in order to convey closely reasoned and finely drawn distinctions. He belongs in the main stream of English prose, whose flowing rhythm and structural simplicity have been influenced by the English Bible to an extent not entirely measurable.

As it was full of parallelism and antiphonalism, Hebrew literature was also characterized by a general tendency to figures of speech and to proverbs. Its vocabulary was ex-

[71] *Moby-Dick,* I, 238.

clusively objective; there were no words comparable to such English words as *principle, relation, contents*. The Hebrews defined an emotion by describing its effect, as Job did when he said, "Fear came upon me, and trembling, which made all my bones to shake. Then a spirit passed before my face; the hair of my flesh stood up. . . ."[72] Ishmael did the same when he reported that he bowed before the albatross.

Thus the Hebrews' only recourse in speaking of abstractions was to use figures of speech. Even in the New Testament, in a chapter like the one in Hebrews on faith, the same method may be seen. Many of the Biblical phrases which have acquired the force of idioms in the English language are the result of this objectivity in description: "the fat of the land," "the valley of the shadow of death." Melville himself could do almost as well. Redburn inquires of a pleasure-loving society, ". . . are we not like people sitting up with a corpse, and making merry in the house of the dead?"[73]

Despite his preoccupation with abstractions, in fact, Melville maintained a surprisingly objective vocabulary. His penchant for bold and explicit figures to represent philosophical and moral truth went far beyond any particular indebtedness to the Hebrews. Yet two of his favorite symbols, it is interesting to discover, were symbols also of Job's: the loom and the mine. "My days are swifter than a weaver's shuttle," cried Job, "and are spent without hope."[74] And as Melville often suggested that truth lay at the bottom of a mine or cave, so Job pictured wisdom as being even more secret than that:

> Surely there is a vein for the silver, and a place
> for gold where they fine it.
> Iron is taken out of the earth, and brass is molten
> out of the stone.

* * * * * * * *

[72] Job 4:14-15.   [73] *Redburn*, p. 237.
[74] Job 7:6.

> But where shall wisdom be found? and where is
> the place of understanding?
> Man knoweth not the price thereof; neither is
> it found in the land of the living.
> The depth saith, It is not in me: and the sea
> saith, It is not with me.[75]

The fondness for proverbs, too, is marked in Melville's writing as it is in the Hebrews'. Their word for *proverb* meant a similarity or likeness. And considering the poverty of both connectives and abstract terms in their language, it is easy to see how they developed the full possibilities of this form. The proverb substituted the concrete for the abstract, and that in a manner requiring but the simplest devices of comparison. Like many authors, Melville quoted the most familiar of these proverbs. But he also constructed his own, putting them now in the mouths of Bardianna and Babbalanja, now of Benjamin Franklin. Just where the Hebrew influence began and left off, both for Melville and for Franklin, it would be hardly possible to say.

To begin with Melville's citations of Scripture is to end with such inherent similarities between the two styles as these of parallel and of proverb. For the truth is that Melville as a literary artist as well as a philosopher had much in common with the Hebrews. Their approach to their material was, like his, subjective.[76] They did not think; they felt. They expressed themselves primarily, and in order to understand a thing they had first to absorb it. Thus, although the Psalmist wrote with his eye on the object, he stood between the object and his readers, and they see it only as it affected him. So nature appears in Melville: the sea is calm or disturbed according to the mood of Ahab; summer at the beginning of the book and winter at the end but reflect the aging spirit of Pierre—they are not seasons of the natural year.

[75] *Ibid.*, 28:1-2, 12-14.
[76] See Duncan MacDonald, *The Hebrew Literary Genius* (Princeton, 1933).

Nor were the Hebrews able to create character apart from their own emotions. In Job, for example, though the stage is set and the cast is ready, there is no real drama; the central character has been completely identified with the poet, and the friends represent only arguments he wishes to refute. It is the same with Melville. The scene on the *Pequod's* forecastle at midnight has all the elements of a play, yet it is instead a grand puppet show, with Melville manipulating all the strings. The protagonist, Ahab, has been utterly absorbed, a fact made all the more noticeable by the presence of Ishmael, who theoretically is Melville.

It is this subjectivity of their thought which is in great part responsible for the irregularity of style characterizing the Hebrew writers. They were incapable of slow labor. Their method was not premeditation but impulse; they never planned, but improvised, striking out flashing phrases and brilliant pictures. The catalogue was for them, as for Melville, a favorite device. Like him they developed their thesis by repetition instead of analysis, a practice which often led them into excesses of language and imagery. The writers of Proverbs and Job did not know where to stop; they had no conception of the eloquence of silence.

This is not so true of the Hebrew storytellers, who were capable of reciting a narrative concisely and quietly. Yet even they could not sustain a chaste style. At times the spirit of the writer seems to become fired by the situation he is describing; the narrative is interrupted while he bursts into song, and not until he has unburdened himself is the story resumed. Familiar examples of this phenomenon in the Old Testament are the song of Moses and the Israelites after crossing the Red Sea and the song of Deborah. Similar lyric poems are also introduced into Melville's prose, now in the form of an interior monologue or soliloquy, again as celebrations of some theme, such as tobacco, ships, kings.

Such phenomena and such *copia* are indeed evidence of a certain kinship which existed between Melville and the

authors of the Bible; an essential congeniality of literary
taste relating them as surely as it did these same authors
and the seventeenth-century prose writers. The fact is en-
lightening with respect not only to his Biblical borrowings
but to the total irregularity of his style. It was not, despite
its appearance, the style of "an irregular innovating genius
who overthrows idols and breaks up a language in order to
build and make anew: he used the things he loved, for they
possessed his mind."[77]

But it was also more than the simple expression of a
subjective mind. As it was his titanic desire to embrace
all oceans and all lands, all ages, and the boundless reaches
of the spirit, Melville also wished to echo all the great and
moving styles of language. A deliberate artistic impulse
moved him to imitate now one and now another. Not one
more than another was the perfect medium, but all were
vehicles to convey the evasive, the wordless and the silent
truth.

[77] John Freeman, *Herman Melville* (New York, 1926), p. 170.

CHAPTER VI

Conclusion

IN ALL THAT MELVILLE wrote he was no nearer saying what he had to say at the end than he was at the beginning. His effect, like Shakespeare's, is one of extension rather than of volume. One receives the impression of spaces and distances, of approaches and retreats, of vistas opened but not entered upon. One is always traveling but never arrives. Structurally there is no end to his tales; they go on and on with the progression of an infinite series. On board the *Pequod* is told the story of the *Town-Ho* and of the *Jeroboam*. Hautia's phantoms and Taji, pursuers and pursued, flee on at the end of *Mardi,* over an "endless sea." "I love an indefinite, infinite background—a vast, heaving, rolling, mysterious rear!"[1] exclaims White Jacket, taking leave of the *Neversink,* with its symbolic name, while it is yet out of sight of land. As the Confidence-Man leads his venerable acquaintance away in darkness, a sequel to his adventures is promised.

Above all, one is made to feel that what has been left unsaid is unspeakably vaster than what has been said. The superabundance of material appals him, and he is driven at last to think of all truth as voiceless and of the question as more final than any answer.[2] "God keep me from ever

---

[1] *White Jacket,* p. 500.
[2] *Billy Budd and Other Prose Pieces,* p. 134; *Mardi,* I, 329; II, 19; *Pierre,* pp. 284, 290.

completing anything," cries Ishmael. "This whole book is a draught—nay, but the draught of a draught."[3]

Had Melville's inspiration been any less inclusive or had his achievement been any more definitive, the irregularities of his thought and his style would be intolerable. As it is, these irregularities are nothing else than the "careful disorderliness"[4] which he declared to be for some enterprises the true method. Not definition is its aim, but suggestion; not keen analysis but bold juxtaposition, contrasts and paradoxes, catalogues and citations, reflections, reminiscences, and reverberations. The sea burns, the sands of the desert "Impart the oceanic sense,"[5] the great cities of the world are wildernesses. Far from being the definitive book on whaling, *Moby-Dick* is prefaced by extracts from seventy-eight other books and contains allusions to scores more in the text. The subject is inexhaustible.

To this desire to extend the scope of his work, to this fear of appearing final, all Melville's rhetorical devices and all his voluminous sources are subservient. So indiscriminately are they introduced and associated that they tend at last to lose their separate identities. They are but fragments of a boundless creation, undistinguished otherwise in the hands of its creator. Of them all, however, no single one so far extends the bounds of what Melville wrote as the Bible. However he alluded to it he was assured of a contrast with his immediate material: between the common and the great, the present and the past, the natural and the supernatural. And though each is a contrast achieved by many other means as well, only this one enabled him to make them all simultaneously, at once magnifying his characters and their affairs, establishing for the briefest moment a background of antiquity, and suggesting the presence of yet another, unseen world beyond the vast scene which meets the eye.

[3] *Moby-Dick*, I, 179.   [4] *Ibid.*, II, 101.
[5] *Clarel*, I, 216.

Originally and essentially, of course, all Melville's material is simple and commonplace, becoming transformed
through a marvelous imagination. Viewed strictly in the
light of fact his characters are of limited powers and lowly
station. Yet as their lives unfold in passion and in problem,
they seem to be supermen, inhabiting a world one degree
larger than life. The effect is deliberate, and it is deliberately more than the general exaggeration of his pen. Thus
did he justify it:

If, then, to meanest mariners, and renegades and castaways,
I shall hereafter ascribe high qualities, though dark; weave round
them tragic graces; if even the most mournful, perchance the
most abased, among them all, shall at times lift himself to the
exalted mounts; if I shall touch that workman's arm with some
ethereal light; if I shall spread a rainbow over his disastrous
set of sun; then against all mortal critics bear me out in it, thou
just Spirit of Equality, which hast spread one royal mantle of
humanity over all my kind! Bear me out in it, thou great
democratic God! who didst not refuse to the swart convict,
Bunyan, the pale, poetic pearl; Thou who didst clothe with
doubly hammered leaves of finest gold, the stumped and pau-
pered arm of old Cervantes; Thou who didst pick up Andrew
Jackson from the pebbles; who didst hurl him upon a war-horse;
who didst thunder him higher than a throne! Thou who, in all
Thy mighty, earthly marchings, ever cullest Thy selectest cham-
pions from the kingly commons; bear me out in it, O God![6]

This effect of magnitude in Melville's characters is
achieved largely by figurative language, since his imagery
contains references to so many great personages of history
and literature. Side by side with the nameless crews of his
ships walk Henry VIII, Charlemagne, Xerxes, Apis, Ammon, Jove, Perseus, Prometheus, Mohammed, Faust, Hamlet, Beelzebub, Abraham. With many of them Melville
briefly compared his own characters: Daggoo and Hivo-

[6] *Moby-Dick*, I, 144.

hitee to Ahasuerus, Jarl at his supper to Belshazzar at his feast, the helmsman of the *Highlander* to Ixion, General McPherson to Sarpedon, the carpenter at his forge to Prometheus, Ahab to Adam: " 'I feel deadly faint, bowed, and humped, as though I were Adam, staggering beneath the piled centuries since Paradise.' "[7]   The Bible, in fact, provides genealogies to ennoble the meannest of men, for all, it asserts in various accounts, are descendants of the Jehovah-created Adam, of the sons of God who intermarried with the daughters of men, of the patriarch Noah, and spiritually of the New Testament Father.   Melville cited them all.

More important than this casual imagery, though, is the deeper relationship which is made to exist between some of these personages and Melville's characters, whereby the patterns of their lives are both clarified and given significance.   Some of them are named for the great, and thus the parallel moves with them: a whaling captain for a king of Israel, a Revolutionary soldier for Jehovah's chosen people, a sailor for the son of a patriarch, another sailor for a Norse jarl, two lunatics for a prophet and an archangel, a religious fanatic for the rebuilder of Jerusalem, a ship owner for an advisor of Job.   Even ships are so titled: the *Jeroboam,* the *Rachel.*   The historical *Serapis* might have sprung from the same fancy, for to Melville the white-sailed naval vessels, like the albatross, the whale, the sky-hawk, were nothing less than archangelic beings.

Appropriately are they called.   For these same characters, as well as others with more prosaic names, wrestle with problems which have preoccupied heroes, sages, prophets, and gods.   They seek the truth in exile and loneliness, in the wilderness of Ishmael and Hagar, of Moses, of John and Jesus.   They pursue the demonic phantom despite testimonies of Faust and Prometheus and Jeremiah that they

[7] *Ibid.,* II, 328.

cannot survive the experience. Some announce with Solomon and with Seneca that the wisdom of this world is equivocal, while others, like Enceladus, Hamlet, Jesus, seek to reconcile it with the wisdom of another, absolute realm. At least one meets disaster through the simple opposition of his nature to evil; Melville found a parallel not only in the Bible but in the lives of Silvio Pellico and Michael Servetus, whose names he penciled in his copy of Fitzgerald's *Polonius*,[8] and of the god Rama, whose riches he declared were "Unmerchantable in the ore."[9]

The speech of these people, too, is appropriate, containing some of the most magnificent of stylistic echoes from the seventeenth century, the Elizabethans, the Anglo-Saxons, the authors of the Bible. The quotations Ishmael makes from Job, Father Mapple's sermon on Jonah, the Confidence-Man's reading from Ecclesiasticus, Pierre's relation of the adulteress's story, Nehemiah's recapitulation of obscure Biblical events, countless echoes of the Hebrew prophets, poets, and sages—all add eloquence to pretentiousness. Like the Teutonic war song of Yoomy and the Shakespearean ranting of Pierre, these words, whether spoken by or about Melville's characters, make each of them seem less and less like a single individual, more and more like Everyman.

It is in just this conception of character, in fact, that the intricate connections between Melville's religious thought, his use of the Bible, and the entire Romantic school to which he belonged are most clearly revealed. Quite likely its belief in the dignity and the possibility of the individual more than all else commended Christianity to him. For this he held to be the great value, the field on which all conflicts were fought, the divinity shaping every end. Man, by the very fact of his being, could be neither common nor insig-

[8] In the Harvard College Library.
[9] *Clarel*, I, 131.

nificant, and often the darkest of skin and the most primitive of mind held closest communion with the heart of the universe.

But it was significantly the Calvinistic and the Lockean elements of this Christian individualism to which he subscribed, not the apostolic or the medieval. It was, in fact, a sublime egotism, at least as much Satanic as theistic, and to no small degree political. Hence all Melville's characters have something in common with the Renaissance and with the Byronic hero. And hence all those in the Bible on whom he depended most to magnify his own were carefully chosen: the ambitious Ahab rather than the repentant David, the rebellious Jonah and the lonely Jeremiah rather than the priestly Isaiah, the aspiring but not the obedient Jesus. For all this is more than magnitude; this is the assault upon the bastions of heaven.

Nor do these characters come alone to Melville's pages. The ancient past to which most of them belong, and which inevitably accompanies them, towers up everywhere, a presence of which he was constantly aware. And again, since none of the scenes of his narratives is older than the eighteenth century, it is largely a figurative method he adopted. The whalemen live together like some old Mesopotamian family. No dying Chaldee had higher or holier thoughts than Queequeg approaching death. Nantucket is the Tyre of New Bedford's Carthage. The pines on the hill are as "lofty archers, and vast, out-looking watchers of the glorious Babylonian City of the Day."[10] Of the civilizations of Egypt and Assyria, whose secrets were just being excavated, he was particularly fond. Describing the first mate of the *Pequod*, Ishmael declares:

His pure tight skin was an excellent fit; and closely wrapped up in it, and embalmed with inner health and strength, like a

[10] *Pierre*, p. 48.

revivified Egyptian, this Starbuck seemed prepared to endure for long ages to come, and to endure always, as now. . . .[11]

"But there is no Champollion," he continues, "to decipher the Egypt of every man's and every being's face."[12] Pierre tells his mother to " 'give that Assyrian toss' "[13] to her head. This earth is "this great quarry of Assyrias and Romes."[14] With such intimations of the earth's age the Bible, of course, abounds; and Melville exploited certain episodes thoroughly: the Creation, the Garden of Eden, the Flood. Sometimes the extent of time is suggested, as when Ishmael is brooding over the dead in the Whaleman's Chapel: ". . . in what eternal, unstirring paralysis, and deadly, hopeless trance, yet lies antique Adam who died sixty round centuries ago. . . ."[15] Again the emphasis is upon the youthfulness of the world at the time of creation. Exclaimed the champion of contemporary authors, in "Hawthorne and His Mosses": "The world is young to-day as when it was created; and this Vermont morning dew is as wet to my feet as Eden's dew to Adam's."[16]

These allusions are the major part of Melville's effort at "oldageifying youth in books,"[17] recreating as they do an ancient background for his narratives. But he also selected certain strategic points in those narratives to "oldageify" and thereby made them discourses upon themes as old as history. An amateurishly half-finished sentence in *The Confidence-Man* affords an example of the difference. Winsome, with Emersonian geniality and Emersonian interest in Egyptology, attempts to convince the Cosmopolitan that Noble is not to be trusted:

"I conjecture him to be what, among the ancient Egyptians, was called a ———", using some unknown word.

[11] *Moby-Dick*, I, 141.   [12] *Ibid.*, II, 83.
[13] *Pierre*, p. 18.   [14] *Mardi*, I, 268.
[15] *Moby-Dick*, I, 44.
[16] *Billy Budd and Other Prose Pieces*, p. 133.
[17] Letter to Evert Duyckinck, April 5, 1849 (*Representative Selections*, p. 374).

"A ——! And what is that?"

"A —— is what Proclus, in a little note to his third book on the theology of Plato, defines as —— ——" coming out with a sentence of Greek.[18]

It finally appears that Charlie is a "scoundrel." The absence of the foreign word emphasizes the purpose of the passage: not to create an authentic atmosphere of antiquity but simply to suggest that the Confidence-Man had been known to history much longer than the nineteenth century, in settings other than the Mississippi River.

So in his first novels, wherein Melville compared the life of the Pacific islanders with the life in Eden before the fall, and in his last, which broaches the doctrine of original sin to explain Claggart's character, the entire sequence of events is thrown backward to the beginning of time. The men of the *Pequod* are engaged in no new business: their vessel bears the name of an Indian tribe as extinct as the Medes and the Persians, and the whales they secure contain the stone spearheads of ancient Indian seamen. As Ishmael puts it: "Who can show a pedigree like Leviathan: Ahab's harpoon had shed blood older than the Pharoah's. Methuselah seems a schoolboy. I look round to shake hands with Shem."[19] Nor does the youthful Pierre confront a new problem: it is older than the Glendinning genealogy, older even than Memnon, Solomon, or the Titans, as old as the inscrutable stones of nature. *Clarel,* too, is an old story. Wherever the pilgrims go they are met by memorials of the first century and of the dateless ages preceding it.

It is this persistent nature of the past, in fact, which is most important in Melville's conception of it. It could not represent escape to him as it could to Schopenhauer, whose sentiment he penciled in *Studies in Pessimism:*

The scenes and events of long ago, and the persons who took part in them, wear a charming aspect to the eye of memory,

---

[18] *The Confidence-Man,* p. 256.   [19] *Moby-Dick,* II, 222.

which sees only the outlines and takes no note of disagreeable details. The present enjoys no such disadvantage, and so it always seems defective.

For the past he saw was not a separate segment of time but an inextricable part of the present, of which the ruins strewn upon the earth are but the most obvious evidence. From them each succeeding age is built, for time, as he consistently personified it, is the mason, not the destroyer. It sets one generation's life upon its predecessor's, as it did for both Hebrews and Greeks: Ahab's upon Jeroboam's, Orestes' upon Clytemnestra's, Pierre's upon Mr. Glendinning's.

Indeed, as every period of the world's history recapitulates all other periods, in each individual exist potentially all who have ever lived. "And like a frigate, I am full with a thousand souls,"[20] muses Taji, dreaming beneath his canopy:

Do you believe that you lived three thousand years ago? That you were at the taking of Tyre, were overwhelmed in Gomorrah? No. But for me, I was at the subsiding of the Deluge, and helped swab the ground, and build the first house. With the Israelites, I fainted in the wilderness; was in court when Solomon outdid all the judges before him. I, it was, who suppressed the lost work of Manetho, on the Egyptian theology, as containing mysteries not to be revealed to posterity, and things at war with the canonical scriptures; I, who originated the conspiracy against that purple murderer, Domitian; I, who in the senate moved that great and good Aurelian be emperor. I instigated the abdication of Diocletian, and Charles the Fifth; I touched Isabella's heart that she hearkened to Columbus. I am he, that from the king's minions hid the Charter in the old oak at Hartford; I harboured Goffe and Whalley; I am the leader of the Mohawk masks, who in the Old Commonwealth's harbour, overboard threw the East India Company's Souchong; I am the Veiled Persian Prophet; I, the man in the iron mask; I, Junius.[21]

[20] *Mardi*, II, 53.   [21] *Ibid.*, I, 345.

The continuity, amounting to actual suspension of time, which Melville thus achieved is something quite different from the passion for experience which characterizes many a romantic, notably his contemporary Whitman. On the contrary, it was as near as he came to surrender of the ego, implying as he did that the world is ceaselessly becoming, that some *élan vital* is at work re-creating every moment anew. Change was more real than permanence, for men as for nations. Existence, in its fullness and its flow, was asymmetric and intuitive.

For in the last analysis Melville considered all recorded history but a fraction of the past, and the cultivated intellect only a part of consciousness. The unexplored regions of the individual and of the racial mind, reaching back into prehistoric mists, beckoned him. Hence he was constantly adding an extra dimension to his scene by suggesting the existence of an invisible world. Man, as Sir Thomas Browne had written, was the great amphibian, destined by nature to live in two worlds. So, indeed, all Melville's men do.

In all that he wrote, in fact, the line between the seen and the unseen is almost indistinguishable. So vast is the universe he depicted that its outermost reaches are well nigh beyond perception: the stars which are to Taji worlds on worlds, the mysterious submarine life at which the men of the *Pequod* peer as they sail through the great armada of whales. Reality merges imperceptibly into unreality. Rather significantly, *Typee* and *Omoo* were followed by *Mardi*, which begins like them as a realistic tale of the sea. But once launched in their boats from the *Arcturion*, Jarl and Taji sail gradually but completely out of the natural world into the "world of mind,"[22] on which the wanderer gazes, it is added, with more wonder than Balboa in the Aztec glades.

[22] *Ibid.*, II, 277.

No less casually and utterly do Ahab, Pierre, and Billy Budd move farther and farther from all that is objective until at last the outward circumstances of their lives mean nothing and the inner significance is everything. Vast as the universe is about them, that within themselves is yet vaster and more mysterious. Pierre can find no twig of thought on which to perch his weary soul; he can build no China Wall in his soul against the barbarous hordes of Truth. The immensity of the Switzerland of the soul, writes his narrator, is not at first comprehended by man, but only by degrees does he gain his Mont Blanc and look over his Alps. " 'O Nature, and O soul of man!' " cried Ahab, contemplating the head of the dead leviathan; " 'how far beyond all utterance are your linked analogies! not the smallest atom stirs or lives on matter, but has its cunning duplicate in mind.' "[23]

Dreams and portents, hypersensitive natures, and miraculous events—these outline Melville's invisible world. Most of them are described with some reference to supernatural phenomena recorded by history and many in terms of Biblical parallels. The visions of Babbalanja and of Pierre have Hebrew, Miltonic, and Greek echoes; clairvoyants such as Tistig, Elijah, Gabriel, the Manxman, the Dansker resemble and even bear the names of Jewish angels and prophets; spectacles of nature, like the whale's peaking its flukes, are in a class with the activities of Dante's devils and Isaiah's angelic beings; occurrences like Macey's death and the *Pequod's* disaster seem to be the fulfillment of prophecies as divinely inspired as Zoroaster's or as John's. Seeing the dead Claggart lying before him Captain Vere exclaims: " 'It is the divine judgment of Ananias! Look! . . . Struck dead by an angel of God. Yet the angel must hang!' "[24]

Like the past and the present in Melville's pages, moreover, these two spheres of existence are not mutually exclu-

[23] *Moby-Dick,* II, 38.
[24] *Billy Budd and Other Prose Pieces,* p. 75.

sive, but constantly impinge on each other. They are synchronized. And as natural circumstances are deliberately compared with supernatural ones, a whole undercurrent of affairs is set in motion. Watching Starbuck visit the sleeping Ahab in his cabin and move to slay him with the musket at hand, one suddenly perceives another sequence of events happening at the same moment in quite another world when the mate is said to be wrestling with an angel. These are no theatrical figures of speech; these are glimpses of a realm more dynamic than any other.

Now in his belief in the existence of this world beyond the world of sense Melville has often been called, and even called himself, Platonic. Like the Platonists, he did believe truth resided in the unseen world of ideas and conceptions rather than in the world of material manifestations. But in his essentially romantic conception of this invisible sphere he was closer to the Hebrews than to the Greeks. Order, rhetoric, and logic did not represent the primal truth to him as did elemental and undisciplined energy.[25]

For the Greeks there was clarity not only in this world but also in the world of gods and ghosts. The gods had a fixed abode, disembodied spirits followed a well-marked course, and converse with both was held naturally and reasonably. In all their mythology there is no touch of fearful novelty. But to the Hebrews this world was vague: except for Jehovah there was no personal identification among spirits, and He had no dwelling place but nature; there was no heaven or hell. And because it was vague it could be very dreadful to them. Whereas the Greeks could watch supernatural beings move among them, influencing their affairs, to the Hebrews such interference was utterly mysterious. It was a blow out of the dark, sudden and unexplained. The unseen world had reached out and smitten

[25] See Duncan MacDonald, *The Hebrew Philosophical Genius* (Princeton, 1936).

the world of sense, writing on the wall at Belshazzar's feast, turning back the waters of the Red Sea, transforming Lot's wife into a pillar of salt.

This strangeness and terror is the chief characteristic of the unseen to Melville. "Though in many of its aspects this visible world seems formed in love," asserts Ishmael, "the invisible spheres were formed in fright."[26] Of the invisible terrors the sea, with the mysterious creatures that pass through it, is the symbol, while the earth is the symbol of the known world:

For as this appalling ocean surrounds the verdant land, so in the soul of man there lies one insular Tahiti, full of peace and joy, but encompassed by all the horrors of the half-known life. God keep thee! Push not off from that isle, thou canst never return![27]

As the sea and the land thus alternate as symbols in his scenes, so the calm and the storm alternate on Melville's sea. For though calmness is sweet and agreeable, the motionless ship is destined to decay. In the rack of the storm it leaps forward, drawing fire from heaven, approaching its goal according as it courts disaster. At the heart of the storm, in the midst of the Great Mutiny, Melville's seekers of truth find and worship it.

This is all in the great tragic tradition of the Hebrews, who regarded the creation, for all its mystery and terror, as the garment of Jehovah. So in comparison with the Greeks they were an optimistic people. The two great tragedians of each race, Prometheus and Job, have much in common: both indignantly accuse heaven of injustice, both assert their own righteousness. But Prometheus, while being consoled by his friends, finds Zeus stern and relentless under a destiny of his own. Job, condemned by men, is driven by his own misfortunes to find in Jehovah the source of wisdom,

[26] *Moby-Dick*, I, 243.
[27] *Ibid.*, I, 349.

power, even of justice. The redemptive power of suffering, to be fully expressed by Deutero-Isaiah and the writers of the New Testament, has its beginning here. From Jacob, who wrestled with the angel and would not let his divine antagonist go until he had received a blessing, through successive captivities the Israelites clung to a Jehovah whose might was more constant than fortune.

For Jehovah was a god who could create both light and darkness, both serpent and dove, who could both ride upon the storm and speak in the still small voice; a god of power equally in realm of righteousness and unrighteousness; who could say to the author of Deutero-Isaiah without apology: "I form the light, and create darkness: I make peace, and create evil: I the LORD do all these things."[28]   And from Isaiah, untroubled by the distinctions of a later sophistication, he could receive adoration greater than fear: "O LORD, thou art my God; I will exalt thee, I will praise thy name; for thou hast done wonderful things; thy counsels of old are faithfulness and truth."[29]

It was with something of the primitive spirit of the Hebrews that Melville, too, was more inspired by this manifestation of greatness than of simple goodness. Many were the passages he marked in his Bible illustrating the unequaled and often curiously demonstrated power of Jehovah: his use of Necho the Egyptian to slay Josiah and of Assyria to destroy Samaria. Many were the verses he checked describing Jehovah's darker designs: "...for who can make that straight, which he hath made crooked?" "... for it must needs be that offences come; but woe to that man by whom the offence cometh!" "He made darkness his secret place; his pavilion round about him were dark waters and thick clouds of the skies."[30]

The picture which emerges from all these suggestions, while hardly that which Melville was made acquainted

[28] Isa. 45:7.   [29] *Ibid.,* 25:1.
[30] Eccles. 7:13; Matt. 18:7; Ps. 18:11.

with in the orthodox circles of his youth, is nevertheless one which must have been closer to his heart. Nothing less than a spirit touching good and evil was adequate to preside over the universe he envisaged. Even in his earliest voyages he found that the green valley of the Typee was, like the Garden of Eden, but a small plot of the earth. And to the end, side by side in the Maldive sea, swam the pilot fish and the white shark, as long before the white whale swam ahead of Ahab while the beckoning breezes blew softly from the green shore. The law which could hang a criminal could also hang the purest of the pure, and that without shattering the universe, but only dyeing its vast sky a deeper rose.

Had the spiritual world of the Hebrews been less elemental or less mysterious, had their thought been less subjective and their style less florid, Melville might not have cited and imitated them so often. For these characteristics were born in him, not derived. Expressed in various forms and in support of diverse theses, they are characteristics which distinguish every great imaginative writer: Job, Dante, Shakespeare, Rabelais, Goethe. The world which they all saw was neither exact nor final; it was the approach, not the end, which they described. All were foresworn never to detain the fairest moment so long as there remained undisclosed Mephistophelian secrets; so long as the path remained hidden "which no fowl knoweth, and which the vulture's eye hath not seen: The lion's whelps have not trodden it, nor the fierce lion passed by it."

It is significant that Melville's persistent image for truth, too, is of something hidden. Ultimate reality exists at the core of this complex universe, at the very heart of its vast reaches, indeed well-nigh impossible to attain for the superficies which surround it. Like Donjalolo "universe-rounded, zodiac-belted, horizon-zoned, sea-girt, reef-sashed, mountain-locked, arbour-nested, royalty-girdled, arm-clasped, self-hugged, indivisible,"[81] it dwells at the center of many cir-

[81] *Mardi*, I, 279.

cumferences. It is a face behind a mask. It is a mummy wrapped in cerements. It is a kernel within a husk. It is deep within a subterranean tunnel. It is at the bottom of a spiral stair. Lucy sees layer on layer when she looks at Pierre. Babbalanja prunes himself: ". . . I will not add, I will diminish; I will train myself down to the standard of what is unchangeably true. Day by day I drop off my redundancies; ere long I shall have stripped my ribs. . . ."[32] Speaking of his own twenty-fifth birthday, Melville wrote to Hawthorne: "Three weeks have scarcely passed, at any time between then and now, that I have not unfolded within myself. But I feel that I am now come to the inmost leaf of the bulb, and that shortly the flower must fall to the mould."[33]

So all Melville's art and all the vast scene it reared are not ends in themselves but means to an end. All his borrowings and all his conjurings are but approximations. They are circumferences of the center, cerements around the mummy, antechambers to the throne room, husks about the kernel. Not truth itself is his culminating vision, but "cunning glimpses," "occasional flashings-forth," "short, quick probings at the very axis of reality";[34] symbolic and fragmentary manifestations of the one absolute, which is in the last analysis inviolable.

[32] *Ibid.*, II, 80-81.
[33] [June 1851] (*Representative Selections*, p. 393).
[34] *Billy Budd and Other Prose Pieces*, pp. 131, 130.

APPENDIX

Moby Dick: Jonah's or Job's Whale?*

THAT MELVILLE made significant use in *Moby-Dick* of both the *Book of Jonah* (containing the most celebrated account of a whale in the Bible) and the *Book of Job* (the classic Hebrew presentation of the problem of evil in human experience) is obvious enough and has often been commented upon by critics. That he consistently represented the "leviathan" of Job as a whale, as it was in popular tradition though it had long been identified by biblical scholars as a crocodile, has been little more than noted,[1] however, and never have his references to the sea monsters in these two biblical narratives been comparatively examined. Such an examination, interesting in itself, is rewarding for the answer it suggests to the central question of the novel: who or what is Moby Dick?

In the *Book of Jonah* the whale is an agent of Jehovah, employed to coerce the prophet to obey the divine will by preaching to wicked Nineveh. This story is the subject of Father Mapple's sermon, which thus early in the novel—even before the *Pequod* puts to sea—presents the proposition that the universe is a moral creation, albeit one of constant conflict between good and evil.

Captain Ahab also adopts this point of view, though he

* Reprinted by permission from *American Literature*, Vol. XXXVII, No. 2, May, 1965.
[1] See p. 14, for example.

differs radically from Father Mapple in identifying Moby Dick as an agent of an anti-Jahovah force. As Ishmael puts it in the chapter "Moby Dick"—the first of the two chapters devoted to defining the object of the novel's quest—Ahab sees Moby Dick not only as the creature which bit off his leg but as the "monomaniac incarnation of all those malicious agencies which some deep men feel eating in them," as "that intangible malignity which has been from the beginning; to whose dominion even the modern Christians ascribe one-half of the worlds; which the ancient Ophites of the east reverenced in their statue devil," as "all the subtle demonisms of life and thought," as, in short, "all evil."[2] In feeling himself the innocent victim of an inscrutable supernatural power, however, Ahab invites comparison not with Jonah but with Job. The parallel is suggested by Ishmael at the conclusion of the same chapter: "Here, then, was this grey-headed, ungodly old man, chasing with curses a Job's whale round the world . . ." (p. 183).

Ishmael's own point of view, set forth in the next chapter, "The Whiteness of the Whale," is essentially unlike Father Mapple's, Ahab's, and that of the author of *Jonah*. Though he compares the fright produced in him by the spectacle of whiteness with "the instinct of the knowledge of the demonism in the world" (p. 192) which frightens the Vermont colt at the scent of a buffalo robe, Ishmael's explanation of his own feeling is that whiteness signifies absence of meaning and even non-existence. To him the White Whale is thus symbolic of a universe which, for all its marvels, is not only amoral but inscrutable—perhaps, indeed, a complete illusion. Excepting the last possibility, it is essentially the view of the universe expressed by the Hebrew Wisdom writers, most notably by the author of *Job*.

[2] *Moby-Dick*, ed. Luther S. Mansfield and Howard P. Vincent (New York, 1952), p. 181. Page numbers are hereafter incorporated in the text.

Indeed, Ishmael adopts that author's conception of the whale (as he took the "leviathan" to be), considered as a species, throughout the novel. The quotation in "Extracts" and Father Mapple's sermon aside, the story of Jonah and the whale is referred to only three times, each time facetiously: when the barman in the whale-head-shaped bar at the Spouter-Inn is called Jonah and when in Chapters LXXXII and LXXXIII ("The Honor and Glory of Whaling" and "Jonah Historically Regarded") Jonah's experience is linked in mock heroic fashion with the feats of Perseus and St. George and the whole argument over its credibility is satirized. Ishmael's references to the sea monster in *Job* are, on the other hand, of serious import, and all convey the awesome tone of the original description. That description comprises Chapter XLI of *Job,* the last, climactic one of the four chapters devoted to Jehovah's reply to Job's complaints about his affliction, and pictures leviathan as uncontrollable by man and without moral value—as, indeed, the whole creation is depicted in all these chapters.

There are six direct references to *Job* in *Moby-Dick,* all but one to Chapter XLI, three of them quotations. They occur in "Extracts," Chapters XXIV ("The Advocate"), XXXII ("Cetology"), XLI ("Moby Dick"), LXXXI ("The *Pequod* Meet the *Virgin*"), and in "Epilogue" (with its quotation from *Job* I, "And I only am escaped to tell thee"). In addition, the name of Captain Bildad may be considered an indirect reference, though as for the biblical Bildad, he, like Job's other two friends, takes the universe to be a moral one, in which good and evil acts are rewarded accordingly. In Chapter XXIV Job is said to have written "the first account of our Leviathan" (p. 108). In Chapters XXXII and LXXXI, Ishmael quotes from verses 4, 9, 7, and 26-29 of *Job* XLI, writing in the first, apropos of beginning his own account, "What am I that I should essay to hook the nose of this leviathan! The awful tauntings in Job might well appal me. 'Will he (the leviathan) make a covenant with thee? Behold the hope of him is vain!' " (p. 131) and in the second, apropos the sperm whale which is fast with three harpoons in him,

In this the creature of whom it was once so triumphantly said— "Canst thou fill his skin with barbed irons? or his head with fish-spears? The sword of him that layeth at him cannot hold, the spear, the dart, nor the habergeon: he esteemeth iron as straw; the arrow cannot make him flee; darts are counted as stubble; he laugheth at the shaking of a spear!" (p. 354)

The reference in Chapter XLI, in which Ahab is said to be chasing "a Job's whale," is of particular interest, since it would seem to be Ishmael's most outspoken disagreement with his captain.

Above all, the cetological chapters of *Moby-Dick* may be considered the expression of Ishmael's *Job*-like point of view. These chapters—some forty-two in all or somewhat more than a third of the total hundred and thirty-five— begin with Chapter XXIV ("The Advocate") and end with Chapter CV ("Does the Whale Diminish?"). They have been both attacked as digressive, especially by early critics but also by twentieth-century ones, like John Freeman, and defended structurally as well as philosophically, notably by later critics like Newton Arvin and J. A. Ward.[3] When they are taken as Ishmael's conception of the whale projected in biblical terms they have a significance hitherto unrecognized. They are to Ahab's pursuit of Moby Dick what Jehovah's reply is to Job's complaints: an oblique denial that morality is inherent in the creation. Like Jehovah, Ishmael

[3] See especially Ward, "The Function of the Cetological Chapters in *Moby-Dick*," *American Literature*, XXVIII, 164-183 (May, 1956).

bypasses the whole problem of evil in human experience, which obsesses both Job and Ahab, and describes a natural world which is neither good nor evil but sheerly marvelous, or in Job's words, "too wonderful for me." Even the tendency toward cannibalism which pervades this world appears thus, by no means the least marvelous aspect of it.

In relation to Ahab's fantastic speeches and actions in the course of his pursuit of Moby Dick, these chapters not only give a sane and factual account of whales and whaling, they imply that Ahab's view of Moby Dick is doubly false, that in the purely natural world no creature is good or evil and no ravener or ravened is guilty or innocent. Unlike Job, however, whose original sense of injustice he shares, Ahab is not brought to change his point of view by any new insight into this world, though his very profession offers him one.

The cetological chapters also represent a correction of Ishmael's own tendency to lose himself in abstract speculation about the nature of the universe and the identity of the self. As has often been pointed out, he is introduced as an outcast, is restored to the human community in consequence of shipping on the *Pequod,* and thus is appropriately the sole survivor of the wreck. His survival is also significant for another reason. The knowledge of cetology which he acquires seems calculated to save him from a fate similar to Ahab's by persuading him of the purely physical nature albeit the endlessly marvelous complexity of the universe. Certainly the mood of wonder, exhilaration, even jocundity, pervading these chapters is in pointed contrast to the horror accompanying Ishmael's periods of metaphysical speculation and introspection. The source of the motto of the "Epilogue"—the words of Job's several servants who escaped to tell him of the catastrophes visited upon him—is thus singularly appropriate, since *Job* also is evidently the source of what comes to be Ishmael's prevailing world-view.

It should be pointed out, of course, that Melville himself did not wholly subscribe to Ishmael's or to *Job's* view of the universe. The shifting point of view in *Moby-Dick,* dominated as it is by the character of Ahab, is evidence enough, without looking at Melville's other works, from *Typee* to *Billy Budd.* As Hawthorne wrote, after conversing with Melville in Liverpool in 1856:

Melville . . . informed me that he had "pretty much made up his mind to be annihilated"; but still he does not seem to rest in that anticipation; and, I think, will never rest until he gets hold of a definite belief. . . . He can neither believe, nor be comfortable in his unbelief; and he is too honest and courageous not to try to do one or the other.[4]

Or, as D. H. Lawrence put it, "Poor Melville! He was determined Paradise existed. So he was always in Purgatory. . . . He was born for Purgatory. Some souls are purgatorial by destiny."[5]

In *Moby-Dick,* nevertheless, the argument seems resolved in favor of a physical rather than a metaphysical universe. Moby Dick is indeed "a Job's whale" rather than Jonah's. The sheer density of the cetological chapters is overwhelmingly persuasive. The unhuman universe in which Ishmael survives, floating on a calm sea past passive creatures of prey a day and night before being rescued, is finally distinguished, moreover, by a profound peacefulness—at least as profound as that of the metaphysical universe in *Billy Budd* on the morning of Budd's execution, when sky and air have first a luminousness and then a clarity of supernatural quality.

---

[4] *The English Notebooks by Nathaniel Hawthorne* (New York, 1962), pp. 432, 433.

[5] *Studies in Classic American Literature* (New York, [1951]), p. 150.

Index

26-27, 34-35, 42, 45-46, 70-71, 137, 169-170; in *Clarel*, 41-45; content, 21-26; faults, 37; secondary sources, 40-41; sensibility, 26-35; structure, 35-41; *see also* Style, Symbolism, Themes

Indians, Melville's interest in, 55-57, 81, 125

Indomitable, the, 133, 135-136

Iron Crown of Lombardy, the, 41

Isabella, Queen, 181

Isaiah, the book of: archangels, 162; marked in Melville's Bible, 10-11, 14, 84, 138, 148, 150; prophecies to Tyre and Sidon, 81 n.; quoted by Melville, 138; seraphim, 163; style, 147, 149-150, 155, 158; quoted, 141 n.-143 n., 148, 155, 159, 167, 186

Isaiah, the prophet: 79, 94, 178, 183

Isaac, 50, 75, 132

Ishmael, in *Moby-Dick*: on Ahab, 61, 64; and Bildad, 72; characterization, 171; cited, 71; and Elijah, 66; on green youth, 114; on the invisible, 185; and Ishmael, son of Hagar, 46-51, 57, 72, 76, 176; moods, 55; on nature, 107-108; quotes the Bible, 11, 108, 140, 143, 146; reluctant to complete anything, 174; rescue, 70, 93; on the sea, 28; on Solomon, 95; on Starbuck, 178-179; style, 167-169; style of apocalypses, 161-162, 164; on whales, 25, 89, 180

Ishmael, son of Hagar: as a character type, 46-59, 76, 78, 90, 104, 176-177; Jonah compared with, 82

Ishmaelites, 59

Israel Potter: Biblical references, 9; dedication, 28; Franklin, 97; source, 61; quoted, 53-54, 128, 167; *see also* Potter, Israel

Ixion, 176

Jackson, Andrew, 175

Jackson, 47, 126

Jacob: accounts of, marked in Melville's Bible, 10; and the angel, 26, 186; at Luz, 26, 102; and Rachel, 70; theophany, 50; whales compared to, 35

Jael, 25-26

James, the epistle of, 138, 146

James, Henry, 168

Jarl: and Belshazzar, 176; and the bread-barge, 29; name, 176, seamster, 143; tattooed, 128; voyage, 182; on Yillah, 24

Jason, 45

Jebusites, 24

Jehoshaphat, King, 62, 64

Jehoshaphat, the valley of, 27, 163

Jehovah: and Abraham, 132; accounts of, marked in Melville's Bible, 11, 186; back parts, 39; chosen people, 176; creator, 176; and the exodus, 49; and Hosea, 85; and Jeremiah, 70-71, 84-90, 149; and Job, 106, 185; and Jonah, 82-84, 89, 111; and King Ahab, 63-65, 67, 80; and King Jeroboam, 66; and nature, 184-185; his nature, 186-187; and Nehemiah in *Clarel*, 142; and New Testament Father, 83, 133, 176; and the prophets, 79, 98, 149; theophanies, 50; throne, 163; and wisdom, 105-111; *see also* God

Jenks, William, 13

Jeremiah, the book of: marked in Melville's Bible, 10, 49, 84-85, 88, 148, 151 n.; prophets lamented, 109; Rachel, 47, 70-71; style, 147-150; quoted, 84-88, 93, 149-151

Jeremiah, the prophet: Father Mapple's use of his story, 84-91; Lamentations by, 11; loneliness, 178; and other prophets, 94; prophecy, 176

Jeremiads, 87

Jeroboam, the: and King Jeroboam, 22, 46, 61, 66-71, 176; and the *Pequod,* 173; and Revelation, 69

Jeroboam, King: and the *Jeroboam,* 22, 61, 66-70; and King Ahab, 66, 181

Jermin, John, 143

Jerusalem: accounts of, marked in Melville's Bible, 11, 14; Jesus's apostrophe to, 109; Nehemiah's plan for, 60, 176; Ruth's tablecloth on, 138; temple, 85-87; Vine's lament, 144

Jesus: accounts of, marked in Melville's New Testament, 11, 14-15, 48 n.,

173; inner law, 91, 94, 112; as an Ishmael, 47; Jacob dreamed of, 26; on Jarl, 143; on Maramma, 115; and Moredock, 125; on Noah, 23; on the *Parki*, 29-30; search for truth, 77; on Serenia, 114, 120; and the stars, 182; Yillah abandons, 86; Yillah menaces, 24

Tamburlaine, 75

Targums, 160

Tarsus, 21, 41

Tartan, Frederick, 52

Tartan, Lucy: easel, 34; fate, 90; and Pierre, 37, 56, 73, 86, 142, 151, 162; and Saddle Meadows, 120; sees layer on layer in Pierre, 188

Tashtego, 64

Teman, 141

Temple at Jerusalem, the: Jeremiah on, 85-87; Melville's reference to, 44, 60

Themes, Melville's: celibacy, 85-86; characteristics, 77-78; Crucifixion, 126-136; domesticity, 33-34, 51, 58-59, 113, 125; the Gospels, 73-75, 112-125; inner law, 85, 87-90; inscrutable nature, 106-108; isolation from the world, 48-49, 51-52, 55-57, 84-85, 125, 129; madness, 52, 110-111; passivity, 128; peril, 88-89; primitivism, 34, 56, 58-60, 112-115, 119-120, 123, 187; prophecy, 65-67, 78-93; spiritual consolation, 83-84, 91-93, 111-112; time, 135-136; trade, 62-63, 81-82; utilitarianism, 71-72, 74, 97-101; wilderness, 19, 34 n., 48-57, 59-60, 87; wisdoms of heaven and earth, 85, 106-112, 114-115, 117-118, 120-122, 125; *see also* Character types, Imagery, Symbolism, names of individual themes

Theocritus, 44

Thorp, Willard: *Herman Melville: Representative Selections*, 3 n., 8 n., 14 n., 39 n., 96 n., 179 n., 188 n.; *Moby-Dick*, ed., 14 n.

Thummin, 29

Timothy, 37

Tistig, 61, 79, 183

Titans, 180; *see also* Enceladus

Titus, 13

Toby, 8

Tophet, 21, 31

Town-Ho, the, 127, 173

Transcendentalism, 77

Tribe, the lost, 54

Truman, John, 102

Tyler, Wat, 35

Typee: Biblical references, 8-9; followed by *Mardi*, 182; imagery, 20, 31 n.; narrator compared with Ishmael, 47; Porter's *Cruise*, a source, 84; theme of the Gospels, 112, 114; theme of innocence, 60 n.; theme of the wisdoms of heaven and earth, 110

Tyre, 81, 178, 181

Ungar, 46, 54-55, 57-59

Uriel, 98, 107

Urim, 29

Uz, 21, 39

Venus, 44

Vere, 72, 130-135, 183

Vermont, 43, 126, 179

Vine, 43, 45, 59, 67, 144

Virgins, the parable of the wise and the foolish, 36, 47, 71

Wagner, Richard, 57

Walker, Henry H., *The Comédie Humaine and Its Author*, 49

Weaver, Raymond, *Herman Melville, Mariner and Mystic*, 12 n.

Weed, the man with the, 102

Wetzstein, Johann Gottfried, 13

Whalley, Edward, 181

White, Viola Chittenden, "Symbolism in Herman Melville's Writings," 7 n.

White Jacket: Biblical reference, 9, 11; quoted 22, 28, 30, 36, 39, 47, 110, 126, 128, 173

White Jacket: cited, 25; as an Ishmael, 46-47, 51-52, 56; jacket, 31; Jesus cited, 128

Whitman, Walt, 182

Wilderness, the: the Hebrews in, 30, 49, 53; Ishmael and Hagar in, 48; Jeremiah on, 87-88, 91, 93; Jesus